Who Shall Be
Educated?

Who Shall Be Educated?

THE CHALLENGE

OF UNEQUAL OPPORTUNITIES

W. LLOYD WARNER
Professor of Anthropology and Sociology,
Member of Committee on Human Development,
University of Chicago

ROBERT J. HAVIGHURST
Professor of Education
Member of Committee on Human Development,
University of Chicago

M'ARTIN B. LOEB
Institute of Child Welfare
University of California at Berkeley

GREENWOOD PRESS, PUBLISHERS
WESTPORT, CONNECTICUT

The Library of Congress has catalogued this publication as follows:

Library of Congress Cataloging in Publication Data

Warner, William Lloyd, 1898-1970.
    Who shall be educated?

    Bibliography: p.
    1. Education--U. S. 2. Social classes--U. S.
I. Havighurst, Robert James, 1900-   joint author.
II. Loeb, Martin Bernard, 1913-   joint author.
III. Title.
[LA210.W33 1972]   370.19   70-138020
ISBN 0-8371-5667-X

Originally published in 1944
by Harper & Brothers, Publishers, New York

Reprinted with the permission
of Harper & Row, Publishers

First Greenwood Reprinting 1972

Library of Congress Catalogue Card Number 70-138020

ISBN 0-8371-5667-X

Printed in the United States of America

To

ROBERT E. PARK

Contents

List of Tables and Figures

What This Book Is About

THE American public schools are, in the opinion of the people of the United States, basic and necessary parts of our democracy. We are convinced that they must, and we hope that they do, provide equal opportunity for every child. This means that those at the bottom can compete through education for life's prizes with those at the top. All that is needed are brains, a will to do, hard work, and plenty of ambition. In our faith every aspiring student may not have a marshal's baton in his knapsack, but in his public schooling he does have an equal chance with everyone else for the White House.

This basic belief in the democratic functioning of our public schools is only partly true. This book describes how our schools, functioning in a society with basic inequalities, facilitate the rise of a few from lower to higher levels but continue to serve the social system by keeping down many people who try for higher places. The teacher, the school administrator, the school board, as well as the students themselves, play their roles to hold people in their places in our social structure.

If the American faith in the public school as a democratic force is to become less fictional, we must examine the relevant facts and determine what distorts this picture. From such information we can gather the necessary knowledge to act intelligently on the problem of who should be educated. This book is about the school's place in our status system, how it must be improved for democratic living, and what it needs to conform more nearly to American ideals.

In the first chapter several children are seen doing the things they ordinarily do and acting according to their environmental demands. The children belong to higher and lower social levels in their community. The things these children learn, we soon see, are powerfully controlled by their places in the status system. To understand how the status-controls operate in the lives of these children it is necessary to know what each status level is like. We therefore present descriptions of the status systems of southern, midwestern and New England towns. We must know what these learning contexts are and how they act as social mazes for the children's learning in order to understand what happens to children when they grow up in America. The American school also reflects the socio-economic order in everything that it does; in what it teaches, whom it teaches, who does the teaching, who does the hiring and firing of the teachers, and what the children learn in and out of the classroom.

The curricula of the secondary schools provide early pathways to success and failure, they operate in a different way on the several class levels, and they are used in a different way by the children of the higher and lower levels. It is apparent that the high-school curriculum is a mechanism which helps perpetuate our class order.

The most significant feature of our status order is the emphasis placed on the social elevators which take the more fortunate up to the social heights and drop the less fortunate to the basement. The chapter on social mobility describes this process. It tells how Americans use such powerful forces as money, talent, beauty, sex, and education to climb from the lower social levels to those higher. The careers of several successful social climbers are analyzed to illustrate how this is done. Their lives provide an informational manual of the "Thou Shalts" and the "Thou Shalt Nots" of the American social climber.

The place of the Negro in our society in many respects is like that of the lower-class white. He has many of the same penalties applied to him and is prevented from enjoying many of the same opportunities as the lower-class white. But there are profound differences between Negroes and lower-class whites which have fundamental consequences for the kind of education provided for them. The problem of race relations is becoming crucial. A whole chapter, "The Negro in the American Caste System," is devoted to analysis of how the education of Negroes works in our caste system.

Because Americans are deeply concerned about increasing the quality and quantity of democratic thought and action and because education is at the core of all our hopes and fears for such improvement, in the final chapter, "Who Shall Be Educated?" a set of principles is stated as a foundation for the betterment of educational methods. Concrete proposals are then offered which we believe are necessary for the advancement of democratic education.

THE AUTHORS

Who Shall Be
Educated?

CHAPTER I

Learning for Living

WHEN the bell clanged out the end of the school day, Miss Crane stood at her desk and watched the boys and girls file out, their steps quickening as they reached the hall. She heard the thumping of feet on the stairs. Her room now was strangely silent and deserted. There remained only the scent of children's bodies. She crossed the room, raised the window, and took deep breaths of the outside air. She had been in the classroom only six hours, but she was tired. She was glad the day was over and that she hadn't had to keep anyone after school.

Leaning against the window frame, Miss Crane looked at the children below without noticing details clearly. She watched them separate out from the crowd at the door. The forces operating on them were the forces of human nature, she thought. The prescribed social lines of the community fell upon them. Boys separated from the girls. Little ones straggled off alone or in twos. Bigger children went off in clusters. Boys in overalls were together. The Polish boys found their own little group, and Polish girls strolled off together. It was as if some force over and above them all had ordered their ways. Their feet were set on roads that would diverge more and more from the common life of the schoolroom. "My, how much they learn that I don't teach them. And how much they learn that I wish I could make them unlearn."

There was Joe Sienkowitz running away from a group of boys who were chasing him. There was Bob Jones from the unruly Jones family. "None of those Joneses," thought Miss Crane, "will come to any good." Katherine Green, her only colored student, walked in dignified loneliness. She was a smart girl but one did not get to know her very well. And as the teacher looked out the window Tom Brown was talking to Kenneth Peabody. "Tom," she thought, "is just an ordinary boy. Nothing complicated about him." Kenneth had been in school until this year and she

remembered him as an ordinary pupil with big ideas, always a
little uncomfortable because his mother dressed him in better
clothes—almost fancy clothes. "It wasn't fair," thought Miss
Crane, "but now he probably is getting along all right. Now that
he is going to a private school. What differences there are among
these children. It doesn't show so much in the classroom, but as
they go out from school each in his own way, you can't help
noticing it. How do they become so different?" Miss Crane would
have liked to know more about them at home. How do they live?
What do they learn at home? What do they come through on
their way to school?

A MIDDLE-CLASS BOY LEARNS TO BE AN AMERICAN

Tom Brown, the ordinary boy, is ten years old and in the fifth
grade. His father owns and runs a grocery store in Hometown.
The family lives in a large, well-kept house in the "better" part
of town. Tom's mother is proud of her home, but she recognizes
that their part of town is inferior to the Hillcrest region where
the Peabodys and families like the Peabodys reside.

Tom's mother belongs to the Women's Club and takes an active
part in civic enterprises. She looks with unspoken envy upon the
few who belong to the Garden Club or the very old and exclusive Fortnightly Club. Kenneth Peabody's mother belongs to both
these clubs. Kenneth and Tom's fathers are members of Rotary
and the Chamber of Commerce; Tom's father is active, and
Kenneth's father pays dues but remains inactive except for the
required minimum attendance at meetings. Mr. Peabody is a
regular attendant of the Wednesday Club, a discussion group in
which the members read papers on literary and learned subjects.
Only the most prominent men in town are members.

The Peabodys are "one of the town's old families," and their
kind are often referred to in Hometown as "our Four Hundred,"
or by those hostile and often envious as "small-town aristocrats."
Tom's mother and father, while respected as pillars of society,
are never spoken of in such terms.

Neither Tom nor Kenneth's father knows or has heard of the
Jones family. Tom's father knows of Joe Sienkowitz's big
brother, who was a great football player, and he says, "That
Sienkowitz boy's football career goes to show how everybody
who wants to, and who tries, can go places in this country." Ken-

neth's father thinks too many people now go to high school. His interest in football is confined to the annual game between Yale and Princeton.

Tom Brown is worth looking at in detail. This is a typical day in his life:

Tom's mother called him at 7:30 and thus began another day. All the days were alike to Tom, except Saturdays and Sundays, when he got up at whatever time he pleased and didn't have to hurry off to school. Tom had learned by now that getting up in the morning was necessary, but nothing very good came of it. All he did was get to school on time.

Tom put on his underwear, a shirt which had been clean the day before, corduroy pants, stockings, shoes, and sweater. He clomped downstairs on his heels and slipped into his chair at the dining-room table. His mother scrutinized him and said, without any particular expression in her voice, "Tom, go upstairs and comb your hair. Wash your face, too."

Upstairs Tom found his older brother Jim in the bathroom sloshing water on his face and neck. Tom dodged past him to get some water in his hands to rub on his face and hair. Then he combed his hair, peeking into the mirror at Jim's side. Neither one said anything.

Downstairs again Tom began his breakfast by eating an orange, then cereal and milk, while rereading the accomplishments of Joe Di Maggio from the cereal carton, and finished by gulping toast and jam. Getting his cap and jacket from the closet, Tom started out for school. He was back in a minute to get his arithmetic workbook and this time he hustled out the door, fearing that he might be late.

Down the street he saw his friend Jack, yelled for him to wait, and they walked along together. About a block from school they heard the last bell. Then they ran but when they reached the school ground it was bare. They walked as quietly as they could up the creaking wooden stairs, hung caps and jackets on hooks outside a door marked 5B, opened the door and walked on tiptoe to their seats, slipped in, took out spelling books and began saying letters to themselves with exaggerated lip movements.

Miss Crane watched them a moment and then said, "Tom and Jack, please stay in at recess time." As soon as spelling was over and time came for arithmetic, Miss Crane said, "Class! Get out your workbooks and work on them while I see where you are."

When she looked over Tom's shoulder, she saw that he was already on page 52 while the rest of the class had not reached page 50. She praised him. "That's fine, Tommy." Tom's cheeks got red, but he worked along, feeling pretty good.

When recess time came, and Tom stayed behind, Miss Crane asked, "Tom, why were you late?" Tom said, "I forgot my arithmetic workbook and I had to go back for it." Miss Crane said, "Don't forget it after this. But I'll excuse you this time. You may go out now."

As he left the room, he passed some girls from his class. One of them asked, "What did Miss Crane say?" "Oh, nothing. She couldn't do nothing to me," and Tom swaggered a little. "Oh, I bet she could," replied the girl. Just then some sixth-grade boys came along and called out, "Who's your girl friend?" Tom turned away quickly and followed the boys down the boys' stairway while the girls went to the other end of the hall and down the girls' stairway to the girls' yard.

On his way home from school at noon, Tom saw Bob Jones, the biggest boy in the fifth grade, and some boys from the seventh grade throwing clods at a boy who ran away on the other side of the street. "You goddam Polack," they yelled, "we'll get you."

When Tom appeared for lunch, Mr. and Mrs. Brown, Jim, and Tom's younger sister, Ellen, were already sitting at the table. Tom slipped into his seat. His mother said, "Tom, how often must I remind you to wash your hands?" As soon as Tom returned to the table Mr. Brown said, "Well, Tom, how did you do in arithmetic?" "Swell!" replied Tom enthusiastically. "Miss Crane said I was ahead of everybody!" "That's fine," said Mr. Brown.

"Dad," Tom asked, "what's a Polack?" "A Polack is not a very nice name for a person who came here from Poland in Europe." "Are they bad people?" "Well, sometimes they are ignorant people and haven't learned American ways."

Mr. Brown left the table and hurried off to his store. He always took a very short lunch hour, as an example to his help. When Tom went out the door, his sister Ellen, seven years old, started to walk with him. "You go ahead, I want to walk with Jack," Tom told her. Ellen walked on alone.

Back at school, the first thing the class did was to salute the flag, which stood in a holder beside the teacher's desk. Tom stood straight and repeated the words of the pledge. Then came geography, and Tom read in his book about Kansas City, the "Gateway to the Southwest." This wasn't very interesting, and Tom rested his head on one arm while he looked out the window.

When the music teacher came in for the music period, she asked the children what they wanted to sing. Several girls waved their hands and told their choices. No boys' hands were raised. Tom's mouth moved with the music, but he didn't know many of the words. At the end, they sang "America, the Beautiful." Tom's face showed life now, and he sang lustily. He knew the words, and the music was easy to sing.

As soon as school was out, Tom and his friends started for a vacant lot, picking up their football helmets at their homes as they went. Two boys, the best players, chose up. Tom was chosen first by one of the captains. Tom felt good. He was getting to be a good player and they knew it. This was the first time he had been chosen first. Maybe he would get a chance to be captain and choose up himself pretty soon.

The game broke up at five o'clock. Tom and Jack walked to Tom's house, where they began to pass the football to each other in Tom's backyard. Tom's big brother Jim came along and intercepted the ball. He kicked it over two fences and said, "Chase it." Tom was mad. "You goddam Polack," he yelled at Jim. Then the two youngsters ran around the house with Jim after them.

When Tom came into the dining room at suppertime he caught his mother's eyes on his hands. He looked at them and saw the soil of the playing field. He hastily scrubbed them and daubed his face with water and came back to the table after the others had started to eat.

Mrs. Brown said to her husband, "Tom used some bad language this afternoon. He called Jim a bad name." "What was it?" asked Mr. Brown gruffly. Jim said nothing, but Ellen, who had been watching when it occurred, said, "I know, he called Jim a goddam Polack."

Mr. Brown looked at Tom, "Don't you ever say that again and, Ellen, don't repeat that kind of language. And, Tom, where did you hear such language?" "Well," said Tom defensively, "when I was coming home from school at lunchtime Bob Jones was yelling that at a boy." "Who is Bob Jones?" asked Mr. Brown. "He's the boy whose father is the janitor of the Odd Fellows Building. He's the biggest boy in my room," replied Tom. "Now look, son, good people do not say things like that. If you want to be like a janitor's son, all right, but, if you don't, you stay away from that kind of boy and don't let me hear of you using bad language again." "I'm sorry, dad, I didn't know it was so bad." When they got up from the table, Tom hustled off to work on his arithmetic before his favorite radio program began. Later, as he turned on the radio, he heard the announcer offer to send a detective badge to every boy who sent in three box tops of Mealo cornflakes. Tom asked his mother if they had Mealo, and she said, "Yes, you have it every morning," and Tom said, "Well, I need three box tops."

About nine o'clock Tom was in his pajamas and ready for bed. His mother came upstairs to inspect him. "Go back and wash your arms up to your elbows and use the brush." When he came back to his bedroom, Mrs. Brown tucked him in and said, "You're a nice clean boy now," and kissed him good night.

Suppose Miss Crane knew all this and more about Tom Brown. Suppose she had similar information about other pupils in her class. Would it help her? She probably would feel a need for some way of interpreting this information so that she could use her knowledge about her pupils to do better teaching. We can give some hints of the kind of interpretation that might be useful.

Miss Crane was right when she said that the children learn much that she does not teach them. She might have added that she teaches them many things unknowingly. The learning that goes on in school is only a part of a child's learning, and even this part is influenced by many things that happen outside the school. Thus Tom's learning of arithmetic in school was influenced by his parents' attitude toward his success in arithmetic and toward his studying arithmetic at home.

Suppose we analyze Tom Brown's day, a typical day in the life of a typical ten-year-old boy, to see what he was learning and how he was learning it. For this analysis we shall need a few simple principles of learning—principles generally agreed to by people who have made a special study of the learning process. To understand Tom Brown's learning we do not need a complicated and controversial learning theory.

The basic principle of learning is that human beings tend to seek pleasant and satisfying experiences and to avoid unpleasant experiences. Therefore they learn to do the things which prove to be pleasant, and they learn to avoid things which prove to be unpleasant. Further, the most general method of learning to get what one wants is by imitating the behavior of those who appear successful in seeking similar goals.

With this simple view of learning we can account for the learning behavior of children in the great majority of learning situations in which they are placed. We can also predict the learning behavior of children in most situations. We cannot account for the finer differences in rate and quality of learning among children, which requires a greater refinement of learning theory than we need in our discussion of social status and learning.[1]

Tom has to be reminded to wash his hands before every meal and at bedtime. He is punished slightly by having to postpone eating for a few minutes and by having to make special trips to the bathroom. He is rewarded slightly for washing "up to his elbows" by his mother's good-night kiss and her calling him "a nice clean boy." This is pleasant but not sufficiently so to establish firmly the habit of washing. It is to be expected that Tom will learn slowly to keep himself clean; the punishments are not heavy for dirty hands, and the rewards are not great for cleanliness. Not until fifteen or sixteen when Tom will want to make a good impression on the girls will he learn to keep himself clean. At that time cleanliness and neatness will be pleasant to him because they will win the approval of girls. Then, we can be pretty sure, his mother will marvel at his care of his hair and his nails and she will wonder how the miracle came about.

There is punishment for being late to school in the form of confinement to the classroom during recess while the other children are out playing. Therefore, Tom is not often late.

Arithmetic is Tom's best subject. Doing well in it brings him many rewards. He wins approval from his teacher; his lateness is excused as soon as he says he had to go back for his arithmetic workbook; his father praises him because he is ahead of his class.

For stopping to chat with a girl at recess Tom is immediately punished by the taunts of the sixth-graders who are just older than he and whom he admires and imitates. Tom is beginning to learn that boys should have nothing to do with girls. Not only does the school put girls on one side of school to play and boys on another, but the boys who have learned to spurn girl companions taunt Tom whenever he is found talking to them. Part of this lesson having been learned, Tom refuses to walk to school with his sister.

[1] All numbered footnotes are grouped at the end of the text, by chapters.

The boys just older than Tom can make life pleasant for him with their approval or punish him with their disapproval. They can permit him to hang around their gang activities and to play sometimes in their games, and if he behaves like them he has a better chance of being accepted. Therefore he is impressed when he hears a group of older boys calling another boy a "goddam Polack." His suspicion that there must be something not altogether right about the boy who is called a Polack is confirmed by his father's statement that Poles are ignorant people—not yet Americans. The principal sources of reward in his life—his parents and the boys just older than he—agree; and he unconsciously learns their attitudes toward Poles.

His father does not agree with the boys on the rightness of calling certain names, he discovers when his father punishes him for saying "goddam." Tom already had inklings of this before. He will be punished for using certain kinds of language in his parents' hearing, but he may actually gain some prestige with his associates by using this same language. He must learn to adjust his language to his audience.

Saluting the flag is an empty action for Tom. He gets little pleasure from it. When he joins the Boy Scouts, however, there may be some ceremony about the flag and Tom may be rewarded by approval of his parents and of other children when he stands with his troop and salutes. Or he may see soldiers marching past the flag, and the next time he salutes the flag he will feel a thrill because he is behaving like a soldier.

Tom is not learning much music. Nobody praises him at home for singing. The other boys do not sing. The songs are not interesting, anyway, except "America, the Beautiful." He likes this song. It is easy to sing. Probably the rhythm gives him pleasure. What is more, this song marks the end of the music period, which is itself a reward. Tom will always like "America, the Beautiful."

For his skill at football Tom gets an immediate reward from the other boys. He will practice passing and kicking for hours, developing more and more skill, because every improvement will be rewarded immediately. If Tom were awkward or puny, his efforts at football might bring him ridicule from his peers and he might stop learning. By being better than average in strength and size, he will no doubt go on playing football, and it will be a source of great pleasure and satisfaction to him.

Tom learns without any difficulty the rules of football and the other games that he plays. The game of marbles, which he plays every spring, has many complicated rules which are no bother at all for Tom to learn. Yet he has trouble with the rules of grammar, which are no more difficult. Tom learns complicated rules of games because he is rewarded for so doing by the other boys. Miss Crane would be astonished at the rate at which Tom would learn rules of grammar if she could find a way of rewarding him as highly as his age-mates can reward him.

Tom learns things largely because he has certain inner needs which demand satisfaction, and because of the approval and disapproval of his parents, his teacher, his age-mates, and those slightly older than he. These are the principal sources of reward and punishment. Other children learn things the same way.

Tom is what Miss Crane calls "an ordinary boy." What about the others? There is "that Jones boy," for instance.

A LOWER-CLASS BOY FINDS HIS PLACE

Bob Jones is one of the younger of nine children. His father is janitor for the I.O.O.F. Building, the largest office building in town except the bank building. It has offices for doctors, dentists, insurance agents, the Federal Farm Security Agency, etc., and on one floor is the assembly hall. Mr. Jones keeps two of his sons busy cleaning the building. The Joneses live in Boxtown, one of the poorest sections of Hometown.

Boxtown's houses are run-down. There are no lawns, and no effort is made to paint or keep the houses in repair. Most of the houses are small. The people of Boxtown have a bad reputation in the community. According to common report by those on the "right side of the railroad tracks," a Boxtowner is lazy and shiftless and without ambition. The county welfare worker told the members of the Women's Club that most Boxtown girls get into trouble because they have no standards. She also said that Boxtown boys are often arrested for stealing from the local merchants. "Their parents are worthless," she said, "and would rather go on relief than work."

One frequently hears about "the Jones boys." They are always getting into scrapes. Mr. Jones drinks rather heavily, and this may be the reason for his nickname, "Corky."

When Bob entered school, the teachers made such comments as, "Well, here is another Jones. Will they never stop coming?" The teachers expected little from Bob, and they didn't get much but trouble. Now in the fifth grade, Bob is twelve years old, having repeated two grades. He is big for twelve and strong and he can, or at least everyone thinks he can, lick any boy in the school. To his classmates he is all that is tough, fearless, and independent. To himself he is just doing what he has learned from his older brothers—he knows how to look after himself.

Bob doesn't want to go to school nor does his father want him to go. What he wants is to earn money. But the school law says school until fourteen. Maybe next year he can get a special permit, like all his brothers, and get a job as a delivery boy for a grocery or drugstore. Bob does not do his homework unless he does it in the detention room after school, to which he is sentenced frequently for some infraction of school regulations.

Most of the boys in his room learned about sex from Bob, who can tell some lurid and sometimes quite incomprehensible stories. Bob's language is imitated, too, by the boys. This special knowledge gives Bob some status among the boys, but during the next year he will lose a lot of that as the children's parents begin to point out what a worthless fellow he is. Tom's father, for instance, told Tom that he shouldn't use such language as "goddam" unless he "wanted to be a janitor's son."

When Bob becomes undesirable socially as well as inadequate scholastically, school will be too uncomfortable, and he will try everything to avoid going to school. The school authorities will give in, saying it is no use trying to stop him from being a truant, and will issue a work permit; and Bob will start on an earning career.

Bob imitates his brothers and his father in dress and speech. If he should shed his overalls and wear his one pair of good pants to school his brothers would make life miserable for him. He will quit school and go to work as soon as possible in order to get some money in his pockets and be able to buy things and do things like his brothers. Thus life will become more satisfying to him.

Bob Jones threw clods and stones at Joe Sienkowitz, and Joe sped home a scared boy. Miss Crane wondered about him.

A Polish Boy Learns to Be an American

The Sienkowitz and other Polish families have a different reputation in Hometown from that of the old American Jones family. The welfare worker, for example, has a good opinion of most of the Polish families. When one of the Sienkowitz boys got into trouble over a minor affair and appeared in court, she came to his aid. She said that his family were poor but honest even though they were foreigners. She told the judge that the Sienkowitzes had a neat little house in a section of the town which was not too good but where people lived well-behaved, respectable lives. All the Sienkowitz children were sent through school. The family was ambitious. By hard work and careful imitation of the Americans they looked up to, they had moved from the edge of Boxtown, where all the immigrant Poles first live, to a region of small houses surrounded by small lawns with vegetable gardens in the back yards. No Sienkowitz had ever been on relief.

The Sienkowitzes go to the Catholic church. None of the Jones family belongs to associations or churches. Joe's father belongs to the Polish-American club and to the Moose. He wants to join the Elks as soon as he can afford it, but first he wants to pay for the lot next to his house.

Joe is getting used to being chased and called names. It happens every day at noon and sometimes in the afternoon. They didn't do it, though, last year when Joe's older brother was around. Joe has two older sisters and two older brothers, one of whom is now away at the State University where he has a scholarship. This brother, Peter, was the state's best high-school football player and is sure to become an All-American. When Pete was around, Joe didn't have to worry because Pete was known to have caught some of the boys and paddled them once when they called Joe names. Pete is big and strong, but Joe is thin and sensitive. He is the baby of the family and having older sisters makes him all the more a baby. The Sienkowitzes are poor—the father works in the factory, and one of the older girls works in the factory too. Sometimes Mrs. Sienkowitz goes out as a cleaning woman to the homes of the better families in town. Joe doesn't work though; all his spare time is spent in learning to play the violin, an hour in the morning before school and at least a couple of hours after school. Joe doesn't mind spending his time this way. His family praises him, and sometimes at school he plays at the assembly. Besides it means that he doesn't have to go through the tortures of being jeered if he tries to play football with his schoolmates. Sometimes Joe thinks of his brother and daydreams about beating up all the other boys, but he has often heard from his mother and sisters and from Pete, too, for that matter, that he must not use his fists because they might get hurt and interfere with his violin playing. Joe's violin teacher is Polish too, and Joe is his best pupil. Next summer, the teacher is sure that Joe can get a scholarship to the special summer camp for musical children where he will get more instruction. Someday—well, who can tell—but someday, Joe will be a great musician. It means, though, practice, practice, practice. Once the music teacher took Joe to Chicago to hear Jascha Heifetz and the Symphony Orchestra. Now Joe can see himself standing with his violin before the great crowd, shining in the bright lights, playing his violin, and then applause, shouts, and encore after encore. It is a long way from being a "goddam Polack" and it is worth the "practice, practice, practice."

A NEGRO GIRL IS TAUGHT HER PLACE

As Miss Crane looked out the window of her classroom after school, she saw one of her pupils go off sedately by herself. Katherine Green was a good student. She was a nice girl—"someone," she thought, "that anyone would be glad to have as a friend except that she is a Negro." Katherine's isolation worried Miss Crane a great deal because there didn't seem to be anything she could do about it. Of course, in any activity which she directed she always saw to it that Katherine took her place, but that did not seem to make it any better. The pupils were not nasty to Katherine—they accepted her as a fellow student but not as a fellow. Nor were all the teachers as concerned as Miss Crane about Katherine and the other Negroes.

Once Katherine went to a school choir practice where they were choosing soloists for a program. Katherine could sing beautifully for a ten-year-old and she was far better than the others. But she was not chosen because the teacher in charge didn't think "it would look good" to have a colored girl sing in front of the choir. Some excuses were made to Katherine, but she knew. She never tried to take part in school activities again.

Katherine's father is a skilled worker in the factory, makes good money, and has quite a good reputation in the factory and in the town.

Hometown was a kind of a way station on the Underground Railroad which took escaped slaves out of the South before the Civil War. Hometown is proud of this part of its history, and there is no great amount of discrimination against Negroes. Though one might not say that the Negroes are subordinated, it is true that the people of Hometown do not just know what to do about them. The feeling about Negroes in America is for the most part too deep-seated to allow taking them as equals without any differentiation. This feeling is enhanced whenever the people of Hometown have contact with others, especially people from the South. So the Green family and the four or five other Negro families who have been in Hometown for two or three generations stay together.

The Greens and most of the other colored families live in neighborhoods which are considered to be nicer than the region where the Sienkowitzes live. Only one colored family lives in Boxtown. None of Katherine or her family's friends associate with this family, for they say, "They are no better than the white trash down there." Katherine and her playmates often visit a near-by town where "there are a lot of colored kids to play with and you can have a good time." Although Katherine accepts and has adjusted to her social isolation by withdrawing from the white children who surround her, she still actively seeks companions among her own people "when they are the right kind."

The men in the Negro families usually acquire a special skill and get good jobs and live most respectably. Most of the children go to high school and some then go on to college or to the larger cities around to get work. As children they play together in their own little groups. Sometimes the boys excel in sports for the school and again they are respected rather than accepted.

As Katherine left the schoolyard she was not being snubbed by the others. They did not purposely ignore her. She just did not belong to any of their groups. When she reached home there were some older and younger Negro children with whom she played. This close contact with older children, plus the responsibility she is given in the home, makes Katherine seem much more mature than other girls her age. Because there are no other Negro children her age and not many who are younger, Katherine always has to take her part in the activities of older children. If Katherine grows up to be like the older girls and boys of her group, she will expect a kind of equality of opportunity in economic affairs but no active participation with whites. In other words, she will have learned to do well what white people do but within the Negro group.[2]

An Upper-class Boy Learns He Is Different

Miss Crane saw Tom Brown walk away from school with Kenneth Peabody. At the football scrimmage Miss Crane would have noticed that Kenneth did not seem to "fit in" well with the group. Kenneth was home for the Thanksgiving vacation period from a private preparatory school in New England. He was the son of Hometown's best lawyer who was the receiver for the town's largest industry. Kenneth had gone to Hometown's school for the first four grades but then his father had sent him away "to get a more suitable education."

Except for the fact that Kenneth, or "Ken," as he was called by his fellows in the public school, had worn fancier clothes, he had always been "one of the boys" when in school. Others had admired him because he was always able to supply equipment for their various games and activities.

A difficulty arose this afternoon when Kenneth objected to the way the others were playing football. They were not abiding by the rules. Kenneth's school had teams for each "form," and they were taught the rudiments of football. The Hometown boys played football as they understood it, and the rules developed as new problems came up. Sometimes they asked older boys to settle their problems and they then learned the correct way, but when they had to solve their own problems they resorted to expediency with much shouting and some show of temper. But here was one of their old pals who wanted the game played his way. It did not matter to them that it might be the right way, it was just that this boy who had gone away to a private school wanted his own way. Each play resulted in some argument and Kenneth often was a third side. Finally, in disgust, Kenneth went home and the other boys were pleased.

None of the boys connected Kenneth's behavior this afternoon directly with his having gone away to school. They had listened to his tales of the good times at his school—the pillow fights in the dormitories, the great amount of sports, the trips the school went on, his teachers, some swell, some funny, some severe, but all different from their own. They heard, too, of the weekend Kenneth spent with his roommate's family at their home on the sea and how he had gone sailing and horseback riding. These were glimpses of a new and wonderful world, comparable only to things they had seen in the movies. It was a life they all longed for—all except Bob Jones, who, meeting Kenneth on the street, jeered, "Well, how is little fancy pants?" and imitated an affected walk, wiggling his hips from side to side.

Kenneth Peabody is being rewarded by his family for wearing nice clothes and speaking proper English. As soon as he is old enough to suffer from the disapproval of his Hometown age-mates for his fine clothes and upper-class ways, his parents remove him to a private school where he finds a new group of age-mates who dress and speak the way his parents want him to dress and speak.

.   .   .   .

Even at the early age of ten or twelve, these children all were traveling different paths in life. The school, with its common life, brought most of them together and gave them a common experience and a common literacy. But, as Miss Crane knew, the prescribed social lines of the community fell upon them and even influenced their learning in school. What a given child learned was not in Miss Crane's power to determine. She could try to teach them all the same things, but they would not learn the same things.

One of the major factors in the choices made for these children by their parents and teachers, in the choices they make for themselves, and in the things they learn in school and elsewhere is their status in the society in which they live. We propose to explore the maze of social status in America to see how it is related to education and to the development of boys and girls.

CHAPTER II

American Status Systems

ALL MEN ARE BORN EQUAL, BUT—

TOM BROWN and the other children of Hometown are taught that in America all men are created equal. They are told by their teachers and they read in their history books that our country is a great democracy where everyone is just as good as anyone else. Despite the teachers and the history books, most of us know that what they say is not strictly true. When speakers from the patriotic societies tell the school children on Memorial Day that we have a constitution which is dedicated to the proposition that all men are created equal and that this means everyone in America is of equal rank, most of us feel that the speakers are telling only part of the truth and that something more needs to be said.

It is obvious that American children are not equal and that they occupy different and unequal statuses. In the present chapter we will examine the kinds of status found in American communities and locate the children and their families in these statuses. We will then have part of the knowledge necessary to understand what these children have to learn to fit themselves to American life.

All societies everywhere, no matter how primitive or modern, have recognized methods for distributing power, prestige, and status among their members. When the social scientist places the simple primitive and the modern complex societies of the world in a range which extends from a pole of absolute equality to the other extreme of complete inequality, a number of things become apparent. The most simple tribes, like the Australian aborigines and some of the American Indians, more closely approach the democratic and equalitarian ideal, while the more complex and modern societies tend to cluster nearer the pole of inequality.

There are reasons for this distribution. In the first place, the simple communities have much less power and prestige to distribute. They have a smaller and more easily handled population.

They are less in need of positions of leadership. Their people are more alike and there are fewer problems of fitting diverse and often opposing groups into compact communities. In order to achieve integrated action it is less necessary to develop social hierarchies which place a few men over the many. The division of labor in many of these simple democracies recognizes differences only between men and women and older and younger people, and it is only among these groups that there are inequalities in power and prestige.

The more complex societies, with their problems of relating large populations, of integrating complex technologies with their task of getting different people such as technicians, skilled and less skilled, tradesmen, professional men, and the members of different religious and ethnic groups to collaborate, must inevitably create places of administration and power which acquire prestige and permit a few men to occupy superior positions over the multitude who are beneath them in power and prestige. The evidence for the relation of social complexity and rank is overwhelmingly strong from all the studies made on the more advanced, nonliterate societies. A striking example of the inevitability of rank in modern societies is the case of modern Soviet Russia. The ideology of communist Russia is democratic and equalitarian. Everyone is a comrade and everyone has equal rank, but the system places the commissars, generals, and other functionaries of the governmental, economic, and party hierarchy above the ordinary citizens. In giving individuals these positions the society thereby unequally divides power and prestige among its people.

Since rank is present in all other complex societies and since the United States is one of the most complex of modern civilizations, it would seem likely that rank should be present in this country. The most casual, critical glance provides ample evidence that we are no exception and the scientific problem quickly becomes one of finding out what kind of social hierarchy we have and of determining whether we have one or many forms of social status. We have researches which have been conducted in the East, South, and Midwest on this problem, supplemented by more casual observations there and elsewhere in the United States, which provide us with some of the answers to this question and the necessary understanding of our social system to answer these questions. Such knowledge permits us to see the demands of our social system and how the system rewards and punishes those who fit into its various parts. We will look at our American social system, which largely controls our behavior, much as we would a complex maze in which animals learn to behave. In such a system we must be taught to learn our way around as we grow up if we are to live normal lives and to behave normally as adults. This is true for all the Tom Browns, Katherine Greens, and Joe Sienkowitzes of our society. Growing up consists in learning how to behave, and learning how to behave means acquiring the proper responses to the batteries of social stimuli which compose our social order.

Class in Yankee City, Deep South, and Midwest

At the outset we can say that these studies of communities indicate that the American status system is not one but a variety of hierarchies. They include caste, class, hierarchies like the factory, church, and school, and unequally ranked ethnic and minority groups. Before we turn to the evidence let us say what is meant by each of these terms.

All systems of rank are status systems in which there are inferior and superior positions. Certain forms crosscut the whole society. This means that the community is divided into several social layers and everyone has a place in one or another of these layers. Other hierarchies segment a society, including some of the people and disregarding others, ordering part of the life of the group but not all of it. For example, a school hierarchy includes a superintendent, principal, teachers, and students among its statuses. Only a part of the life of the community is included, and only a part of the life of each individual who is in a given status is controlled by the school hierarchy. Tom Brown the student is also Tom Brown the son, the brother, the playmate, and one of the children of the community. The status "student" is in the school hierarchy, which is a segment of the total system. High or low status in the school hierarchy does not necessarily imply high or low status generally in the whole community.

On the other hand, when we speak of the upper, middle and lower classes of England, we thereby include everyone and all the life of the community. Class and caste are systems of rank which crosscut the community and include everyone. Social hierarchies, such as the factory, the school, the church, the associations, and similar institutions, are segmentary and include some and exclude others. Ethnic groups, aggregates of individuals in the community who are socially organized by a variant social tradition from the usual one, may or may not be ranked in superior and inferior positions. In the United States we tend to place "foreigners" in places of inferiority.

Class is present in a community when people are placed by the values of the group itself at general levels of inferiority and superiority and when the highly and lowly valued symbols are unevenly distributed among the several levels. Social mobility in a class system permits an individual during his lifetime to move up or down through the several social strata. A man may be born lower-class but in time climb into the upper ranges of the society, although ordinarily a person stays in the class into which he was born. Class rules also permit an individual to marry outside his own level as well as within his social group. A man or woman can marry above, below, or in his or her level. A class structure, then, is flexible, and there is always movement in it.

Caste, found in many parts of the world in addition to India, is a rank order which classifies all the people and all the behavior of the society. Like a class order it unequally distributes the things which are prized and those not wanted. But here the resemblance between caste and class ends. Where class approves of outmarriage, caste prohibits it. A man must marry in his own caste, for the rules forbid and custom punishes marriage outside the caste. There is another major distinction between the two: whereas class positively sanctions and rewards efforts to climb from a lower social level to a higher one, caste disapproves and punishes such behavior. The rules of caste demand that an individual be born, live, and die in one caste.

In the American communities studied and reported on in this and the chapters which follow, a class system and other hierarchies, such as economic and political ones, are found. In some a caste system was reported present. Before discussing these several rank orders, let us briefly describe each of the communities.

Yankee City is a New England community of about 17,000 population. Although formerly a shipping center, it is now an industrial city whose chief manufactures are shoes and silverware. The town is one of the oldest in New England. While possessing a number of ethnic groups, its dominant social tradition is Yankee and what is called Old American. The several ethnic traditions are being modified to fit the older Yankee one. The society is stable and the social change which occurs is comparatively slow and has not disrupted the established system.

Old City in the Deep South also is stable and possesses an old tradition which has been slow to change. It is a town of over 13,000 and is the market center for the cotton counties which surround it. Its population is over 50 per cent Negro. It is not an industrial community and possesses few individuals who are not American-born.

Hometown in the Midwest is a small town of a little over 6,000 people in one of the states not far from the Mississippi River. It is a market center and has a few important industries. Like all midwestern communities it was more recently founded than Yankee City and Old City. Its life is stable and settled. A number of ethnic groups are among its inhabitants.

These communities are not mere satellites or suburbs of a larger city; they have a life of their own. Their people feel that they run their own affairs and identify their lives with their town. There are certain variations in the social hierarchy but basically the class levels are similar. The New England community has three social classes, upper, middle, and lower.

Each class is redivided into higher and lower levels. The same is true of the Deep South. Midwest shows less clear class differentiation than towns in the South and East, but the general outline is similar. The status terms used here refer to social levels recognized by the community. They have no moral implications. It must also be stressed that the several levels are something more than economic categories; they include *all* aspects of the lives of the individuals at each level. Particular emphasis is placed on the kinds of organizations to which individuals belong, and in general their way of life.

Since the class structures of these three communities are similar and because the Yankee City class characteristics are more fully documented, to save time we will use the data from that community for the class description.

Yankee City

The name applied to the upper class of Yankee City is Hill Streeter. The term refers to a "higher class part of town." The name of the upper-upper class is "old family." An upper-upper man believes himself to be a gentleman, and his wife knows that she is a lady. These convictions ordinarily carry a security which people impart to their children along with a pride in their family background and the illustrious lives of their forebears. The upper-upper people are separated from the lower-upper by knowledge of a lineage in which high social position in Yankee City can be traced back for several generations. This aristocratic lineage, which is traced through the father and mother but preferably through the father, is given the name of "old famly" when the members of a class are identified and separated from the lower-upper and upper-middle classes. The upper-uppers ordinarily live in large and well-conditioned Georgian houses which are along Hill Street or in extensions of Hill Street. The houses of the upper-upper and the lower-upper classes, which are the most important symbols of high status, are the most expensive in Yankee City. The two upper classes pay higher rent than the classes below them.

The upper-uppers are professional men or proprietors of the larger business and industrial enterprises—the highest brackets in the occupational hierarchy.

The old family group comprises but 1.4 per cent of the population, has many more women than men, a smaller proportion of young men and women than any other class, and a higher proportion of old people. They marry later than any of the other five classes. There are many maiden sisters and unmarried daughters living in the old houses who seem content to maintain the old homes and gardens and carefully nurture the family traditions while their brothers and other kindred go elsewhere to earn a living or gain renown in their professional careers.

The Hill Streeters attend the Episcopal and Unitarian churches and consciously avoid the Catholic churches and such Protestant ones as the Methodist. The minister of one of their churches must be a strong man and of the right class if he is to maintain his own ideas. He continually feels strong social pressure to say "the right things." No man could long keep his pulpit who preaches a social philosophy antagonistic to the prevailing one of his parishioners. It is possible for him to say things in his pulpit which are considered "a bit daring," but to do this he must have made strong affirmations which have classed him as a minister with "good hard sense."

It should be remembered that the ranking of churches in the United States varies regionally and locally within the major areas.

In the Midwest and the South it is the Holiness and Pentecostal churches which are filled with the lower classes. In southern communities the Methodist churches are often preferred by the local elite, and the Congregational church sometimes is ranked as socially superior.

In Yankee City the upper-upper people participate in associations which are social clubs where topics of interest to the group are discussed. Such interests include history, biography, science, the *ritual* objects of the house and garden, and outdoor activities. The upper-uppers join with the two classes below them to give charity to the lower groups but refuse to allow these recipients to be members of their charitable organizations. They thereby effectively subordinate the takers of their gifts who cannot return these favors and who feel and are felt to be unworthy of admittance to these "organizations of the people who live in the big houses on Hill Street."

In Hometown the distinction between old and new families is not clearly drawn. The town is too small and too young for such distinctions. The Peabodys are clearly members of the upper classes in Hometown. When one learns that they are referred to as "one of our fine old families" and that Mr. Peabody inherited his wealth and his prestige from his father who had a substantial inheritance from "the first Peabody," we know that they are at the top of "the small-town aristocracy." Scrutiny of the characteristics of Tom Brown's family reveals that they are not. Later we shall see that they have most of the characteristics of the upper-middle class of Yankee City.

The lower-upper person in Yankee City (his class makes up 1.6 per cent of the population) is without a recognized lineage for Yankee City since his family is socially "new" and in the final sense of the word he does not "belong." He feels this and must compensate for it, for example, by living in perfect houses which are furnished with the most antique of antique furniture and surrounded by perfect gardens. He tries to give the best parties, to own the finest cars, or become the best in a particular sport or in some other hobby, or become highly recognized in the arts or in some other form of social accomplishment. He continues to try to reach the top, but he can never quite succeed for his judges are his own competitors and those who hold the places above him. Furthermore, the game is stacked against him since he has never had and can never get the one card he must have above all others—gentle birth. Only several generations of living can remedy this matter for him. This he knows, sometimes consciously, sometimes unconsciously, but refuses to admit. His struggle goes on, for after all it is better to advance slightly, or maintain his place, than to go down and feel the ridicule of those of his own class and the mockery of those who are his social betters. He recognizes himself as a gentleman, but he knows that he is not completely accepted as one by those who "really count."

The upper-uppers are strong supporters, with a few noteworthy exceptions, of the right wing of the Republican party, but their convictions are tempered with some skepticism about the reasons for their beliefs, and their "liberal education" has made them aware of other points of view which their secure social position allows them to express but not to feel. The lower-uppers are emphatically Republican by vote and by deep conviction; so too are most of the members of the upper-middle class. Those of the lower-upper class who have rebelled from the rule of their elders are anything but Republican, preferably radical, but these young rebels reverse the position of their elders to demonstrate their freedom from the hateful rule of an inferior upper class which their fellows have accepted in practice.

The lower-upper class shares the old Georgian houses with the upper-upper class. Their houses, like those of the old families, have their own lineages which, by the very listing of the names of their occupants, tell a story of superior status and of better living. If one cannot have a family with a lineage one can buy and maintain with proper respect a house which has a superior one. Furthermore, one can buy a house which is on Hill Street, whose very name symbolizes social superiority and fine living, which places one at least geographically near and, it is to be hoped, socially "near" the old families. Such hopes as these maintain a behavior which, in the generations that follow, ultimately places these new families in the maturity of time among the old families; and in retrospect these present ancestors will rise in the memories of coming generations from new families to old families. Sometimes, to make sure of this, their successors will actually dig up their bones since they are now those of an "old family's" ancestors and remove them from the more common cemetery and place them in a "better location" in a graveyard where the better people bury their dead. When the sons of their offspring perform this symbolic task they will follow the simple precedent not only of those of their own class but of those families in Yankee City which now feel securely placed among the other old families. All the old families of today were the new families of yesterday.

The upper-middle class, comprising 10 per cent of the people, is a superior group of Side Streeters (they are said to be at the side of and not on Hill Street) and are sometimes thought of as "Homevillers." Sometimes the highest of the upper-middle class people may be pleasantly surprised by being classed as Hill Streeters by those of less knowledge in the lower classes. The upper-middle class is not fully "socially acceptable" to the two upper classes, but its people are said to be "the good people" and "the respectable people." The manners and tastes of its people are not fully developed in the class sense. There are subtle distinctions in its speech and deportment at the dinner table and elsewhere which the subtle eye of an upper-class Yankee, particularly if *she* be a native, will notice immediately. In their behavior with those above them, there is a certain giving of precedence by the members of the upper-middle class, there is a masked deference to the words, beliefs, and precepts of the superior classes which helps these middle-class people to gain social acceptance in the larger associations of the upper classes, such as the Women's Club. They are sometimes felt to be "a little vulgar" and not always sure of "how to do the right things." Not all of this class are mobile; many of them are content, and "these good people" are often the respectable community leaders who are "the salt of the earth" to all classes. This is so because, to their inferiors, "they don't put on airs" and, to their superiors, they are "sound and thoroughly dependable."

The great majority of the homes of this class are medium in size but some are large. The upper-middle people are largely Yankee, with a sizable representation of the Irish and a scattering few of other ethnic groups, such as the Jews and Italians. They marry later than any class below them and at about the same age as the lower-upper class.

They belong to the Protestant churches and not to the Catholic churches. They join such churches as the Congregational, Baptist, and Christian Science, but not the Episcopal or Methodist. Most of their children go to the local high school, and only a few of the more socially ambitious parents send their children to preparatory schools.

The Browns of Hometown clearly fit into the upper-middle

stratum. They belong to the right kind of associations, live in the right part of town, and Mr. Brown is a leading businessman in the community. Mr. and Mrs. Brown do not belong to the social clubs of the Peabodys, but they do belong to some of the better civic organizations which include people like the Peabodys.

The upper three classes, which compose about 15 per cent of the population, look upon the lower-middle members as "respectable" but "belonging to the masses." Some of them are Homevillers but "the little people" of that area. They are Side Streeters who are in the kinds of organizations where "you never see them." Those who are below them know they are Side Streeters and not Hill Streeters, despite the fact that the lower classes often place the members of the upper-middle class in the Hill Street group.

The lower middles (28.4 per cent of the total population) are felt to be the top crust of the lower half of the society by those beneath them, by those above them, and by themselves. The lower-middle class people live in medium- and small-sized houses which are not in the best condition, and are located nearer "the wrong part of town." Their houses are worth far less than those of the three classes above them, but still they are worth considerably more than those of the two classes below them. Their property holdings are also far below the upper three, but again they are well above the lower two classes. They are employed in large numbers in the retail stores.

This class has a smaller percentage of Yankees than any of the classes above it. The lower-middle class people marry younger than any of the classes above them and older than either of the two classes beneath them. They belong to the Protestant churches but not to the two Catholic churches.

No class above the lower-middle belongs in significant numbers to fraternal organizations or to auxiliary associations; in fact, these classes avoid such organizations. But the lower-middle class membership is significantly high for only these two types of associations. There is here a sharp break in the kind of participation the classes below upper-middle enjoy in Yankee City. Furthermore, all the classes above lower-middle are members in significantly high numbers of charitable organizations and social clubs, but the lower-middle class and the other two beneath it are excluded from or avoid such associations.

It is in the lower-middle class that the increase in number of arrests is first noticeable. They account for 8 per cent of the arrests of Yankee City. This is four times as much as the upper-middle, but only one-third as much as the upper-lower class. The juvenile arrests are far higher than those of the upper classes and much more like those of the two lower classes. It is in the lower-middle class that such organizations as the Society for the Prevention of Cruelty to Children and the truancy officers are able to take effective action in the control of children and to interfere with the role of the parent in the family system.

The members of the upper-lower class are always grouped with the masses by those above them, by those below them, and by themselves, but they are seldom called "Riverbrookers," for they are above them. They are the largest class, having 33 per cent of the population.

Half of their houses are small and less than one-seventh in good condition. The great majority of the upper-lower class are semi-skilled workers, and over 80 per cent are above the level of un-skilled labor.

The upper-lower class has a greater percentage of ethnic members and a smaller percentage of Yankees than any other class in Yankee City. Only the lower-lower class marries younger than the upper-lower class. It has the smallest percentage of Protestants and is the only class which shows a preference for the two Catholic churches. Only the lowest class has a higher rate of arrest than the upper-lower.

Joe Sienkowitz and his family would fit into the upper-lower class were they in Yankee City. They are mobile ethnics who have climbed out of Boxtown (Riverbrook in Yankee City). While they are poor and "little people," they are not at the bottom of the social heap.

All other classes look down on the lower-lower class. Its members, before all other classes, are of the masses. They are River-brookers ("from across the tracks," or "Boxtowner," or their equivalent). They are "at the bottom" of the lower classes. The lower-lower class people live in the poorest houses in Yankee City and in the "worst areas" in the community. More of their houses are small and in bad condition than of any other class. Their houses are located in areas which are considered the worst in the community. They pay their rent by the week and less than all other classes.

Over 60 per cent of their people are laborers. More of them are unemployed than all other classes.

The lower-lower class, with 26 per cent of the total, is the only one which has more males than females, and it leads all others in number of children. It marries earlier, has a larger percentage of juvenile members, and more married people than other classes. In Yankee City its people prefer the Catholic churches, the Presbyterian, the Methodist, and Baptist churches, and they avoid the Episcopal and Unitarian churches. They join and avoid associations in about the same way as the upper-lower class.

The lower-lower class is easily the most vulnerable to police interference; 65 per cent of all the arrests in Yankee City are from this class and about 11 per cent of the members of the lower-lower stratum have been arrested. About one-third of the arrested individuals are adolescent. Its family life is more disturbed by the police and its parents are more coerced by the private associations.

The Jones family have all the characteristics of Riverbrookers. The Boxtowners, the Riverbrookers, and their like are found in all American towns; and in most communities they are concentrated in areas which have names indicating lowly status.

It is evident from the foregoing that the several superior and inferior classes of Yankee City, with new and old Hill Streeters at the apex of the hierarchy, with the Homevillers and Side Streeters in the mediate statuses, and the Riverbrookers at the bottom, show a recognition, even if democratically disguised, of a rank order in their lives. Each class in Yankee City is an evaluated way of life in which the several parts tend to conform in value to the general place of a class in the rank order. The class order of Yankee City is a system of interconnected statuses which systematically places the thousands of individuals who live in it and thereby provides these individuals with a coherent way of life.

The Peabodys, in an upper-class status, the Browns, in the upper-middle class, the ethnic Sienkowitzes, in the upper-lower, and the Joneses, in the lower-lower class, all belong to the white race and are socially placed by our class order. But the life of Katherine Green and the lives of the other colored people of Hometown are controlled by another powerful status system which socially isolates and subordinates them. We must postpone consideration of their problems until a later chapter.

Deep South

The class alignment of the whites of the Deep South is similar to that of Yankee City. The rural cotton economy places greater stress on rural occupations than industrial ones. The top two classes are an "old aristocracy" (upper-upper) and people who are "aristocratic" but not "old" (lower-upper). Below them is an upper-middle class who speak of themselves as "people who should be upper class" and are referred to by the upper class as "nice, respectable people" and by some of the lower-class people as "folks with money."

Those in the lower-middle class sometimes call themselves "we poor people"; the upper class say they are "good people but nobody," and the lower class say they are "way high ups but not society." The lower classes are classed as "poor whites" and "no-count lots" by the upper and upper-middle classes. The upper-lower people speak of themselves as "poor but honest" as compared with the "shiftless people" below them. The lower-lower say they are "people just as good as anybody," but others are likely to refer to them as "pore white trash."

Midwest

In the Midwest also the class system is present but, as said previously, not quite so definitely marked as in the Deep South and in Yankee City. Several other midwestern communities have been observed, and there are indications in each of a number of social layers. There are definite upper, middle, and lower classes in each. Perhaps the best evidence at present does not come from the scientific studies so much as from novels such as those written by Sinclair Lewis, Theodore Dreiser, and Booth Tarkington, which have interpreted the social life of the towns and cities. Lewis clearly marks several social strata in his novels *Babbitt* and *Dodsworth* when he describes the social life of Zenith. In *Babbitt* he describes Babbitt's efforts to develop social contacts with the McKelveys and the attempts of the Easterbrooks to raise their social level to that of the Babbitts. Babbitt and his wife failed to get into the social cliques of the McKelveys, and the Easterbrooks are not successful in their efforts to climb into Babbitt's group. The McKelveys are "new rich in society," but they are not as high as the Eathorne and Dodsworth families who are "aristocracy and old family." Babbitt is the successful upper-middle class business-man, and Easterbrook is the less successful lower-middle class businessman. The Dodsworths are products of eastern colleges, Babbitt and McKelvey of the state university. The workingmen of Zenith are below the level of the Easterbrooks and their like.

SOCIAL CLASS IN THE FORTY-EIGHT STATES

The question must have arisen in the reader's mind about how general this system of ranking, found in the above communities, is throughout the United States. Is it to be found in the Far West with all of its emphasis on one man being as good as the next? Is it true for all parts of the South and the new parts as well as the old? Is it in large metropolitan as well as rural areas? And if it is elsewhere in the United States, what are the comparative rankings among classes who occupy the same relative positions? Would an upper-middle class Midwesterner rank equally well in Deep South and Yankee City? It is with these questions that we will now be concerned.

The size of the community, the region in which it is located, the rapidity of growth, the type of growth, and the degree to which its older traditions have held are potent factors in the strength and power of the American class order. Let us see how each contributes to this type of system found in the several communities of this country. We will first examine the question of size. All large American cities have their social registers and Blue Books which separate the "people who count" from all the rest. All of them have their areas which are "the wrong side of the tracks" and others believed to be "the better districts." This much is clear with no further inquiry. The novelists contribute further evidence. Several modern novelists have described part of the class system of Philadelphia with its top "Main Line" and the several strata below it. We remember how in *Kitty Foyle* Kitty did not marry the man she loved because the social distance between them was too great and could never be bridged. Boston's Brahmins and the other higher classes have been carefully analyzed in such novels as John Marquand's *The Late George Apley*, *H. M. Pulham, Esquire*, and in William Dean Howell's *The Rise of Silas Lapham*.

Similar indications of class differences in cities in other parts of the United States could be given. A more careful scrutiny of the material, however, indicates that there are decided differences in the class system found in smaller cities and towns. The inhabitants of the smaller places view their community as a whole. An individual knows or "someone he knows" knows everyone in town. A man's background cannot long remain unknown, and almost everyone is socially placed. This is much less true in the great metropolitan areas. Here a family can move from one section to another and establish new social connections without everyone's knowing that they have raised their social status. On the other hand, social contacts are less easily made for the same reason and consequently the problem of raising the family's status is increased because it frequently is impossible to make the proper connections with the people above them.

A large city is much more developed and has a greater variety of people in it than a small one; the social differences are much greater and it seems likely that the lower-class people are further removed from those at the top than the same social level is in a small town. The different class levels tend to associate more with their own kind, but the interconnections of the several layers are not so clearly marked as in the small city where everyone's knowledge about everyone else tends to place people socially and restrict the possible range of their class participation.

A town or city which has been recently established and had a rapid growth in population has not had the time to establish a stable social system. The state of flux prevents the formation of a definite class order. An upper-upper class built on the foundation of lineage is impossible. Consequently a lower-upper class founded on new wealth striving for old family recognition and prestige is impossible. An upper-middle class and a lower-middle class may develop, but no clear demarcation is likely between them, just as it is unlikely that there will be one between the lower-upper and the upper-middle. The keystone of the stable class structure that is firm and resistant to destructive forces is a strong, old family society at the top. Therefore, very new cities and towns, old towns with recent growths which have inundated the original population and broken its social system, and old communities which by growth have changed their ethnic composition are communities which have a more open and fluid system of power and prestige.

A brief survey of a few of the cities and towns in two regions of the West will illustrate this point. On the West Coast, San Francisco and Los Angeles are highly contrasted. Los Angeles has had the most rapid development of any of the great cities of the United States. It has grown from a town of 6,000 in 1870 to a community of several million. Most of this growth has occurred in the last twenty years. The original social system and its carriers have been destroyed. The rapid technological, economic, and social changes combined with the conflicting cultural background of people from the South, Midwest, and Far West have kept the status system in flux. The older Spanish-American status hierarchy clings to its distinctions. The early Anglo-American population has largely lost its social traditions and the new unstable Hollywood society with its so-called "caste distinctions" bears a closer resemblance to the occupational hierarchy of a factory than to a class order. All the elements of class are present except social stability and maturity.

In contrast, San Francisco is a more settled and stable community. It has grown more slowly and its population and social shifts have occurred within the social framework early established. The upper classes are more clearly demarked. This is less true for the metropolitan Bay District which surrounds the city itself.

The California large towns and smaller cities conform to the same rules found in the two large cities. Small stable communities tend to have more marked status distinctions. The small towns which service a large rural area which have had late industrial development maintain a status hierarchy that is easily observed. The new industrial communities do not.

There are even more marked differences between old and new communities in the East and South, since these areas have had time to develop more closely integrated social systems. On the whole, the small cities and large towns of the Deep South and New England have a more clearly defined class order than those in the Midwest and Far West. Their old families tend to be more respected than those from the other areas of the United States. A Chicago upper-class family, recognized as at the very top in that area, is felt to have made a good marriage for one of its sons or daughters if the young person marries into an upper-class Bostonian family. The prestige of Harvard for the "sons of successful men" in the other areas of the United States is founded not on its scholarly worth alone but upon the solid strength of the aristocratic Boston and New England families who attend it. The club system for the young men in the university reflects the class system of their elders. There are not many wealthy New York families whose sons have sufficient social prestige to be acceptable to such organizations. There are still fewer eligibles from other parts of the United States. The "newly rich" and the "socially prominent" of Chicago, Kansas City, and Detroit who go south and east to buy old mansions and estates recognize the superiority of the eastern and southern class system and try to play the hardest social game where the rewards are higher and more stimulating to the daring.

The rural areas of the United States, composed of working farmers, seldom make clear distinctions of rank between the social levels. Today, with easy transportation available, the people in rural areas tend to be dependent upon the larger communities around them for their social distinctions and to fit into such a pattern.

In brief, the small cities in the oldest regions with the least social change in their histories tend to have the most clearly developed class orders; the youngest areas with the greatest social change have the least clearly developed social classes but the chances of social mobility are greater.

CHAPTER III

Social Mobility—Going Up and Coming Down

How to Make the Grade

THE two most important factors of a class order, we have said, are upward and downward movement for an individual or a family and marriage above or below the class of the individual. This creates a fluid condition in the social hierarchy that may be "open" and make social mobility easy or it may be "closed" and mobility becomes difficult. Wealth, income, and occupation are important factors in our class system, yet the possession of great wealth, a large income, and a highly placed occupation do not ensure such a fortunate individual the highest class position. They are important symbols of prestige and arsenals of social power, but by themselves they are not sufficient to give their possessor certain top position. On the other hand, they are sufficient to prevent him from occupying one of the lower rungs of our social ladder.

A man may be the head of an important factory, have a large income and bank account, but he may not necessarily be a member of the upper class of his community. The first generation of a wealthy family is usually not in the highest class. It is necessary for an individual and the members of his family to acquire other symbols of prestige and to participate on the basis of equality, or partial equality, with members of the higher classes. Some of the symbols necessary include the acquisition of outward personal behavior including manners, etiquette, and speech habits which are enforced by inward attitudes and values which have become habitual to the individual. Other necessary symbols are a personal and a family environment which symbolize higher position. These include houses, furniture, and similar symbols of status to increase the strength of his claims to higher position.

All this means that a mobile person's money must be translated into a way of life which expresses high status. Such behavior is not sufficient, since, to be rated at the top, it is necessary for him to participate in clique, associational, and often family relations before he is securely placed. These conditions are of greater importance to a woman than to a man. A man is more often forgiven his manners than a woman her etiquette. Wealth is not the only elevator whose power can be used to establish social position. Talents of all kinds which are highly prized raise their possessor's position and make it possible for him to acquire the other necessary symbols and to establish the relations essential to participation in the higher social ranks. A talent for music, singing, painting, acting, writing, or athletics, as well as many other activities, gives the individual prestige in his own profession which may be translated into social position. A rise may or may not be accompanied by the acquisition of wealth.

TALENT AND OCCUPATIONAL MOBILITY

A young woman of Yankee City of upper-lower or lower-middle class parentage had an ability to write fragile, extremely lyrical poetry. She early received recognition from the critics, and her verse was accepted by the better poetry magazines. The increase in her income was much less than that of many of her age-mates who had become secretaries to businessmen. She never achieved economic independence by her writing, but always had to do more menial jobs for her support. The poetic talent gave her direct relations with a number of people of social prominence who admired her poetry. These relations gave her an opportunity to learn how to behave and to increase her participation with her "social betters." Marriage to a member of New York's upper class entrenched her as a permanent member of the upper group.

An artist who quickly made a success as a writer for the popular magazines and thereby greatly increased his income easily converted his money into "better living" and in time was accepted by people much higher in the social scale than the lower-class position to which he was born. But his large income did not give him the same high social acceptance as the young woman who came from lower levels than he and made no money by her talent. On the other hand, a member of an old family developed a talent for writing cheap fiction, filled his pockets with money, and in so doing added to his prestige and was accounted a clever fellow. Talent in all three of these cases was important in elevating the social position of the possessor—to the first, income was of no importance; to the two latter, it was of considerable importance.

Occupational mobility in a hierarchy such as a factory, school, or church usually contributes to the general social advancement of a man and his family, but this is not always true. A teacher came into the Midwest from the outside. His family could have been little better than lower-middle class. While teaching, he continued his college work and after a number of years he advanced through the school hierarchy to the superintendency of the city's school system. During this time he and his wife had lived modestly and knew few people. When he became superintendent, he met the members of his board, among whom was a man from a lower-upper class family. He was occasionally invited to this board member's home to talk over school affairs. One evening he was asked to bring his wife. In their efforts to find a common meeting ground the two wives discovered that they were members of the same sorority. This gave them common identification and increased their feeling of nearness. The superintendent's wife in time met the friends of the other lady and was invited to join two of her clubs and became a member of her clique. In a few years the superintendent and his wife became members of the board member's social set. During this time they had bought a "nice house" in "the better part of town," exchanged their furniture for that acceptable to the new group, and had taken over the attitudes, values, and much of the outward behavior of the new social level. Most of this they did without being too conscious of it. They had arrived socially in the lower-upper class, where they were considered the social equals of the others, and like their new friends they participated, though not as equals, with members of the old family level.

Here we have a case of successful mobility in the restricted school hierarchy being translated into successful mobility in the larger class order. The latter success does not necessarily follow the former often because the individual or his family may be unable to convert his prestige and power within a segmental hierarchy into general acceptance in the class order.

In a near-by town a parallel case of occupational mobility was observed. A lower-middle class teacher who had come to the town had worked his way up to the superintendency. He was married when he arrived to a girl whose beauty had attracted him. She had come from the wrong side of the tracks and was of

Polish ancestry. Her schooling had stopped after graduation from the commercial course of her home-town high school. He had been considered a good match for her by her family. His family had felt her to be beneath him. When the husband had been appointed to the superintendency, the extra money had enabled them to buy a new home and to live better. He met some of the more important men in the town. He joined the Rotary and made speeches at several important events. But, although they met "the right people," they were not accepted. She was under criticism for her "crudities," and he for not knowing how to get along. They did not succeed in translating occupational success into general class mobility.

In the same school system as the first superintendent's were two teachers who were middle-aged, not beautiful, and dressed in an ordinary manner. They occupied ordinary positions as teachers. These same teachers were acceptable in all of the "right homes" because they came from the town's old families. They received a certain deference from the superintendent and his socially conscious wife because they knew the general class situation of the two. Here we have a situation often found in school, church, factory, and other American segmentary hierarchies. The top status in a segmentary hierarchy may be occupied by an individual who does not enjoy the highest social position, while a low status in the same hierarchy may be filled by someone from a top social position. If adequate accommodations are not made by the individuals involved, these distortions may result in conflict among them.

MOBILITY BY EDUCATION

Education, as one of the most important elevators, takes a great variety of forms in helping or hindering social mobility in our American status system. The successful college graduate prepares himself for a career as "a trained man" and tries to ensure a better place for himself and his family than that to which he was born. The career of the scholar, a combination of education, talent, and occupation, is often a clumsily disguised success story.

Alton Danverse was the son of a lower-middle class hardware merchant who had a corner shop in a New England industrial town. He was a younger son whose older brother terrorized him. He clung to his protecting mother and, encouraged by her, turned to his studies. As he grew to adolescence, he collected Indian relics with a boy from a near-by city. To both of them it was an escape from harsh reality. In their hunt Saturday afternoons they met a well-known archaeologist from one of the great eastern universities. Alton became an informal assistant to the professor on his field trips. When he graduated with only a B average from the local high school, the professor got him a scholarship to his university.

During his four years at college Alton had little social life. He knew socially none of the young men who were in the clubs and fraternities, but he met a few of the younger sons of the Brahmins in his classes in Egyptian archaeology. They often sought his company and his notes just before examinations. At graduation, with some small help from his protector, he won a research fellowship and went to Egypt. While on his first "dig," he met the daughter of one of the more powerful New York families who was taking a Grand Tour. She was not beautiful. In fact, she had been referred to as the ugly duckling of the family and had been reared so carefully that she was said to be a prude. Alton's lack of masculinity and aggressiveness and his almost feminine ability for light conversation at the personal level appealed to her. When they later met in New York, they saw much of each other and three years later became engaged. This occurred after some protest from her parents. Alton meanwhile had been appointed instructor in the Department of Oriental Studies. Alton ultimately was accepted by her family. Through his wife he met the members of the old families. Alton was with them but never of them. Later in his life his three daughters were not counted as Danverses but were reckoned in the mother's family line. They all made successful marriages at the social level of their mother.

Alton Danverse had succeeded in translating successful educational and occupational mobility into elevation into lower-upper class status. His children did not fall to his own level. Like Alton Danverse's rise, the social mobility of most people is usually propelled by a variety of factors. His personal habits were partly responsible for his acceptance as a husband, which contributed to his ultimate rise in the class hierarchy. The social analyst is often able to select what factor is most powerful, but sometimes it is difficult.

Another favorite mobility route is through good works. This occurs at all social levels. A man makes money and the family translates this into better living. His wife gives to charity and interests herself in worthy enterprises where she participates with people above her. From the restricted and limited "internal" participation in charity organizations, she extends her relations with those who are above her, and her activities include most of the things they do. Churches and associations are used for these purposes at all levels from the lowest to the highest classes. If mobility is successful, the steps taken move from church or large association which has representatives from all social levels to smaller and more restricted associations over to cliques which have only the intimate friends of the higher people in them.

Sex and Beauty

Beauty is often a powerful factor in elevating the social position of women and sometimes of men from lower to higher social rungs. It has contributed to the statistics of more women marrying up than men. Beauty may be thought of as a word which directs our feelings in two ways. It is often associated with stimulating sexual interest, and it is thought of in an artistic context which helps disguise its sexual meaning.

Mary Dodowsky was a Polish beauty. Her father and mother were laborers in a shoe factory. At sixteen, after an affair with an older man of some prominence in the community, she took the $300 he gave her and went to New York for a career on the stage. Her long legs and firm breasts and clean-modeled face appealed to the casting director of a swank night club. He liked her both for his chorus and for himself. After two years in the chorus, during which time she was kept in the director's apartment, a talent scout from Hollywood saw her. She had a screen test and spent a weekend at Atlantic City. The talent scout said she had great possibilities and gave her the money to pay her way to Hollywood. When she returned to the apartment, she packed the expensive wardrobe the director had bought her and left for Hollywood without saying good-by to her protector. The talent scout came on the next train because he had once had a minor threaten him with charges based on the Mann Act.

For two years Mary Dodowsky was mauled by Hollywood, but her striking beauty almost always worked to keep her supplied with a man who was financially responsible for her. One day the owner of a large chain of picture theaters came to the lot where Mary had a role as an extra. He spoke to her and said he thought she had screen possibilities. He asked her to come to see him. Mary's beauty had given her sufficient experience with older men to teach her how to act when she saw him in his private office. He was not young and was afraid of old age and death. She made him forget his age. During their ripening intimacy she was skillful in eliminating the embarrassments older men sometimes experience under such circumstances with younger women.

Mary was given training for the stage, which prepared her for the increasingly important parts she was getting and for acting her new role as the lady of the house in a Beverly Hills mansion. In time Mary was starred. She never acted well before the camera, but her behavior in her new home was excellent. After a number of rebuffs when her protector attempted to introduce her in Hollywood outside the motion-picture society, Mary persuaded him to divorce his wife and marry her. They then moved to Long Island where he built a magnificent mansion. Mary bore him several sons. She gave to church philanthropies and contributed liberally to the better charities. Despite this and their efforts to become one of the Long Island group, they were not accepted. After an humiliating experience, they went back to Hollywood. Here they occupied a top position as celebrities in the Hollywood hierarchy.

Mary's career of beauty is a story of both success and failure. She gained her goal of money and fame and lost her bid for social success because it was said she was not acceptable. During Mary's rise to stardom, Elizabeth Dryden, from an old New York family and a famous beauty even before her coming out party, came to Hollywood. At that time she was married to a man in New York who was of her own social status. Gossip columns carried hints of a coming divorce. She was seen with the same prominent director who had been her escort in New York before she came to Hollywood. Their friends said that the gossip was unfair, and they declared that the love of the two was most idyllic and that the lovers showed great courage to bow to the demands of love. After each had secured a divorce, they were married. Elizabeth had been starred in her first picture. Despite the gossip which a few called a scandal, her eastern friends continued to visit her and her husband. Only a few of her former husband's friends broke with her.

Elizabeth Dryden was said to be respectable and she was accepted. Her moral behavior did not interfere with her rise in the

Hollywood occupational hierarchy. Mary Dodowsky was not respectable and was not fully accepted. Further analysis reveals that Mary Dodowsky was considered vulgar and her manners synthetic. On the other hand, Elizabeth Dryden was felt to be a lady. The basic difference between the two women was the social level from which they started. The beauty of each provided the power for increasing her prestige. Mary's beauty carried her a greater distance than Elizabeth's, but Mary had a longer distance to go. She never reached her destination. Elizabeth had no distance to go in class position. She merely moved up in the motion-picture hierarchy. Mary's beauty was powerful enough to permit her rise from the bottom of our society to where she was near the top. Her "vulgar" background was too heavy a weight for her beauty to lift over the final class barriers.

The Social Rise of Flora Belle

The history of Flora Belle tells how apparent frigidity gives some women the necessary equipment to climb all of the long route up rather than being stopped by emotional attachments to men they know on their upward journey. Her climb to the top was achieved by the use of beauty as a stimulus to attract men of higher status followed by astute manipulation of the social groups in which she participated. Some have said—they were her later friends—"It shows what education can do." Others—they were her onetime friends but present enemies—replied, "It's all according to what you mean by education."

Flora Belle is a beautiful woman. When she was a high-school girl and walked down the street, her well-formed figure was a cause of much comment and occasional whistling when she passed the boys on the corner. While such attention annoyed her, she felt disappointment when no one gave her this mark of sexual approval. Flora Belle has reddish-brown hair, beautiful fair skin, large brown eyes, and small features. She is about five feet, three inches tall, slender but well developed. She is often described or complimented as the "Vivien Leigh" type.

Flora Belle was a leading light of the high-school crowd. In her senior year she won academic and social honors in school and was "engaged" (going steady) with the most promising boy in town. Flora Belle went on to college, for which all her family sacrificed as did Flora Belle herself; money was borrowed from the bank; and Flora Belle worked summers.

At college Flora Belle quickly found that she was not going to be rushed by the better sororities. Only the socialites got bids to the good ones. She determined to stay out of the poor ones because joining them would keep her down all the time she was in college.

Flora Belle was elected to all the student organizations as a representative of the "Barbarians." In these organizations she discreetly cultivated the friendship of the girls from the better sororities. By the end of her sophomore year she was in a clique of sorority girls but maintained close connections with the socially powerful girls who were not in a sorority. By this time she was a leader of the nonsorority girls. In her junior year she was asked to join one of the most important sororities. As soon as she was initiated and not before, that is to say, when she felt socially safe, she snubbed her old friends in the nonsorority group and campaigned against a girl, who formerly was her best friend, in an important school election.

Flora Belle successfully used this cold-blooded method of upward progression the rest of her life. When she entered a new and socially higher group, she continued her relations with the older and lower one until such time as she knew she was secure with the leaders of the new top group. She then dropped the old and lower group and, with the aid of the leaders of her new clique, formed friendships with girls at a still higher level. In time she dropped those who had aided her but not until she was certain of her new position. In other words, she kept one foot securely on the step below until she was sure the foot above could carry her social weight at this higher level, then she raised the backward foot to a step still higher and thus continued her upward journey.

During the summer vacation after graduation, Flora Belle was notified of having been accepted for a teaching position in Old City. She went as soon as possible to Old City to get a place to live. She canvassed the various places where schoolteachers lived, but carefully picked the house in which her new school principal lived. During her first few months, she spent most of her social life with the other teachers, playing bridge and in discussion groups of one kind or another. Ruth Watson, the principal, took Flora Belle along with her to some entirely different kinds of social affairs. The parties to which Ruth had entree were the upper and upper-middle class affairs, because of her contacts with the school administrative and P.T.A. people. By midwinter of the first year, most of Flora Belle's social life was with these people and little of her time outside of school was spent with her fellow teachers.

Flora Belle was a great success at parties—she had a ready wit and was charming, especially with men. Her attitude toward intimacy with men was cold. She confessed to Ruth Watson, "Well, a fellow takes you out and you go to a nice place and you have a good time and then he expects a little loving, so you've got to give it to him. I don't get a kick out of that sort of thing." She never betrayed sex interest in any man who courted her. She made all of them feel uneasy and a little ashamed. They believed her unattainable and therefore highly desirable.

Flora Belle soon "gave up for good" her home-town boy friend as she was keeping steady company with Bill, handsome upper-middle class son of Lawyer Ramsey, chairman of the Board of Education. After her first year in Old City it was generally understood that Flora Belle and Bill would soon be married. It seemed that Flora Belle was much in love with Bill, but to Flora Belle as to other girls in her set in Old City Garnet Ainsley was the most eligible man.

Garnet Ainsley was born in Old City. He is a member of an old plantation family. He is in his late forties and lives in his father's old colonial home. He and two sisters inherited a small fortune. Garnet's older sister lives in the fashionable section of Memphis. He is a member of the best clubs and country clubs. Garnet Ainsley has all the characteristics of a "refined, southern gentleman."

Early in the autumn of her second year in Old City Flora Belle was invited to a dinner party at the home of Mr. Matthews, one of the city's leading business men. The "best people" of Old City were there and Flora Belle was escorted home by Garnet Ainsley. During the autumn Garnet Ainsley had a couple of dates with Flora Belle, although she was most often with Bill Ramsey.

During the Christmas vacation, Ruth Watson visited a sister in New Orleans. The day after Christmas Flora Belle appeared without warning saying that she was just on a visit. However, Flora Belle remarked casually that she had heard Garnet Ainsley was in town. Ruth had not been aware of this and arranged that they all get together. Garnet Ainsley took Flora Belle to a grand New Year's Eve party.

Back in Old City for the winter, Flora Belle had more frequent dates with Garnet. Soon Flora Belle was wearing a diamond that was the talk of the town. The remainder of the school year Flora Belle and her family were all frantic—corresponding, telephoning, and visiting—to get the Bennett home remodeled for the wedding in June.

After her marriage, Flora Belle entertained a group entirely different from the one she ran with the previous year. One of her former friends, a teacher, said, "I don't see how Flora Belle can be so indifferent. I didn't think she would." And then she showed her resentment—"If it were not too mean, I'd tell people in this town how her mother, who was a wretched orphan, was brought up by some not very nice people. Wouldn't many people lift their eyebrows at that?"

Flora Belle even ignored Mrs. Matthews, at whose home she first became acquainted with Garnet Ainsley. In one instance Flora Belle said that she "could not afford to invite Mrs. Matthews to this dinner party as she did not fit in."

Shortly after the birth of her second child, Flora Belle wrote to Ruth, "Garnet gave me a set of stone martens and I feel like Mrs. Richbitch when I wear them. Some friends have invited me to spend a week in New Orleans in January. I am planning to leave the babies, husband, and house for a whole week. It will be fun if I can stand it."

Flora Belle, as her father stated, "has always got what she wanted," and certainly this characterizes her life story. Though Flora Belle may not be very happy in her upper-upper class position, her children will certainly be comfortable "at the top."

Flora Belle, when looked at objectively, is a hard, calculating woman. She is always looking out for a way to climb the social ladder. One gathers from her confession about sexual matters that she is cold sexually and that sexual activity is one way and a good one to get ahead in the world. Furthermore, she has little affection for her children, except as they prove that she is really the wife of Garnet Ainsley and the matron in his home. Flora Belle's life is full of maneuvers to get ahead and she views every aspect of life from that angle. The teaching profession has been invaluable to Flora Belle on her upward path. Perhaps no other profession could suit her purposes so well.

It must not be supposed that all social mobility is unashamed and purposive and conscious social climbing. Some of it is, much of it is not, and some of it is even unwillingly done. The man who makes money because he is interested in his job and finds himself, because of his new power and his good works, meeting people and belonging to groups he had no intention of knowing is often in this category. He may be resisting the loss of his older and less well-placed friends and grudgingly accepting the advances of his newer friends. The lawyer or doctor who rises to prominence and prestige and, because of his new position, is accepted by the associations of his highly placed clients, who no longer frequents the society of his lowly placed former friends, is often a man who fights being socially mobile. Despite this, the society itself places him at higher social levels.

The few thumbnail sketches given in this chapter illustrate some of the more usual forms of upward social mobility. The variations on each of these themes are beyond count and almost inexhaustible.

Downward mobility is less easily observed. The facts are often hidden or disguised because the unfortunate participants feel ashamed of them. The most frequent factors are loss of money, loss of place in a school, church, association, economic, or other hierarchy which contributes to taking away the individual's social place, refusal to obey the rules of etiquette and morality demanded at a particular level, loss of talent, "bad marriage," ineptness in using social rituals, lack of education commensurate with the level to which a man is born, conflict with the powerful people in one's social group (such as clique, association, or church), and psychological maladjustments which will not permit proper social adjustment. In other words, downward mobility happens to those who have not attained a secure position in any social class.

Upward and downward mobility are part of the social system provided by a class order. The route up and the route down are complex and composed of a vast variety of factors, some of which are powerful and, for certain kinds of mobility, necessary—others are less powerful and not always necessary.

The implications of the American status system for education are great. The remaining chapters of this book will be concerned with some of the important aspects of the problem. We will see how the curricula of our schools often conform to class requirements, how status operates to help or hinder learning, and how the teachers and school administrators fit into the caste and class structures. We will examine the life careers of several teachers to find out what happens to them in such a system.

CHAPTER IV

The School in the Status System

NEW SOCIAL RESPONSIBILITIES OF EDUCATION

IT IS a truism that the school system must fit into the machinery of the social order. The school is a social institution; as a social institution it must do its part in making the society "work." The school system in America has developed from a minor cog in the simple machinery of the simple society of the early Republic to a major set of gears in the complicated machinery of the modern social system.

Benjamin Franklin was the tenth son of a Boston candlemaker. At an early age he was apprenticed to a printer. He educated himself by reading anything he could lay his hands on in the shop where he worked. All told he had about two years of schooling. When he was seventeen years old he went to Philadelphia and arrived there with a Dutch dollar and a copper shilling in his pocket. Within a few years he was well-established in the printing business. With a passion for improving himself and others, he soon became a leader in public affairs. In his spare time he studied the new science of electricity and soon was sending descriptions of his experiments to the Royal Society of London, where they were eagerly read by the greatest European scientists. He was commissioner to France during the crucial years of the American Revolution. Back in Philadelphia, he aided in the fight to adopt the new Constitution which united the thirteen colonies into the United States of America. During his lifetime he rose to the highest social positions.

Abraham Lincoln was born in a Kentucky log cabin, the son of a wandering farm laborer. He went to a backwoods school long enough to learn the three R's. Altogether his attendance at school did not exceed one year. He grew up in the hills of southern Indiana and on the prairies of central Illinois as a rail-splitter, a flatboat man, and a clerk in a general store. He educated himself and became a country lawyer. He went into politics. He developed a good law practice in Springfield, Illinois. He ran for the United States Senate and was defeated by Stephen A. Douglas. In a time of national crisis he was elected president. As President of the United States he carried the nation through a disastrous Civil War, won the confidence of all kinds of people by his moral greatness, and died when his task was done, universally recognized as a great man.

Upon these stories and many more like them the youth of America have fed their minds. The United States of America was the land of opportunity. A whole generation of youth read the books of Horatio Alger, which repeated over and over again the American doctrine that any boy who was poor, honest, industrious, and ambitious was "bound to rise."

Equal opportunity to all—that was America's promise. It was on the lips of every preacher and schoolteacher. It was taught at every humble fireside. Every businessman, industrialist, and politician proclaimed it and believed it.

The promise was heard in Europe everywhere during the nineteenth century. It was heard by starving Irish bog-farmers, Norwegian fishermen, the poor in Polish ghettos, German artisans, weavers in Lancastershire, Bohemian miners, Italian peasants. It was heard on the other side of the world by Chinese coolies and Japanese farmers. America—the land of unbounded opportunity! They came, surging waves of immigrants, for eighty years. Ships carried them to Boston, New York, Philadelphia, and Baltimore. The railroads carried them west. Ships carried them to New Orleans, where they took stern-wheel steamers up the broad Mississippi and up the Ohio and Missouri, populating the great Middle West. Ships carried them to Seattle, Portland, and San Francisco, where they peopled the cities and cultivated the fertile river valleys.

This polyglot collection of humanity, with diverse folkways and physical appearance, became a unified nation in an amazingly short time. There was actually more unity among the Irish, Scandinavians, English, Bohemians, Germans, Poles, Italians, Serbians, and Greeks in America than there was among the Irish in Ireland, the Poles in Poland, Germans in Germany, or Italians in Italy. Foreign-born Americans were largely unconscious of the tie that held them together and united them with native-born Americans. But we can see now that this tie was their common belief in the existence of equal and unlimited opportunity which made it possible for any person with ability and character to rise in the world. "In the United States you can raise yourself up," they said. With one accord they distrusted anyone who preached class consciousness. They believed in America and so created a society that was vigorous and confident of its future. They were certain that everyone in America could be sure of a fair deal.

It was evident to all that America offered equality of opportunity, because so many people rose from humble beginnings to high places. As long as upward social mobility is so common that everyone can observe it all the time, people will believe that opportunity is equal and plentiful. If upward social mobility becomes less frequent, if the common man sees fewer people rising in the world, belief in the existence of equality of opportunity fades. In spite of the possible argument that people at the bottom of the social heap are born with less innate ability and therefore cannot expect to rise, the ordinary man is apt to diagnose a lack of social mobility as a lack of opportunity.

The social mobility of nineteenth century America has been explained by sociologists and historians as due to three causes— cheap land, expanding frontiers, and expanding business and industry.

There was plenty of good land to be had at a low price for the labor of clearing, plowing, and planting. Little capital was required—no more than could be saved in a year or two's work or advanced by an ordinary man from his savings. Immigrants, younger sons, and disgruntled city workers could always move out to the frontier and be sure of a fair reward for hard work. Those who were foresighted and industrious could count on growing wealthy as the West developed and could be reasonably sure of placing their children at the top of the social pyramid.

Business was usually good, and industry was always growing. Great new industries developed: lumber, meat-packing, flour-milling, steel, oil—then chemicals, electrical products, and automobiles—and finally airplanes, motion pictures, and radio. There was always room at the top in the ever-expanding industry of the country.

During that century education played only a small part in promoting social mobility. The elementary school made people literate, but family, church, and community gave young people the character which fortified their native wit and made them push ahead. High school and college provided avenues of mobility for a few who rose thereby into the professions of medicine, law, the ministry, and teaching. But this was a narrow pathway compared with the broad highway provided by agriculture, business and industry.

Social mobility continued to be the outstanding feature of American social life on into the twentieth century. Although the frontier had disappeared and the good land was all taken, business and industry continued to grow. The postwar business boom of 1920-1930 may have accounted for more upward economic mobility than occurred in any other decade in the country's history.

But by 1930 a change had come over the pattern of social mobility. The preceding few decades had seen marked increases in the number of people in the technical and service professions. Chemists, engineers, teachers increased greatly in numbers. Anyone aspiring to these positions needed general education and special skill. Native wit and perseverance were no longer sufficient. The collapse of business expansion after 1930 put the finishing touches on a picture of social and economic mobility that was entirely different from the nineteenth century picture.

The People Turn to Education

A study of high-school and college enrollments tells what the American people did when it became clear that education and special skill were needed more and more for social mobility. Before 1890 attendance at high school and college was confined to less than 5 per cent of the youth of the country. These were mainly boys and girls of high social position and economic status who were being educated to take the places of their parents, together with a few lower-status boys and girls who aspired to high status and chose to secure this higher status by entering a profession.

The schools and colleges began to grow rapidly during the period from 1890 to 1910, and they expanded with almost explosive velocity from 1910 to 1930. Within a period of fifty years, the proportion of young people attending high school multiplied tenfold, and the proportion of young people attending collegiate institutions multiplied three- to fourfold.

Still believing that their children should rise and seeing in the secondary school and college the principal avenues of mobility, the people sent their children to secondary school and college. The American people learned what the people of older cultures have learned, that the schools are the social elevators in a hardening social structure. The Chinese have known this and used the schools in this way since the time of Confucius. In Europe the school system represents a social elevator moving from the very bottom of a society to its top and has been used for this purpose for a long time.

At great sacrifice American parents struggle to put their children through high school and college. They want their children to "have an easier time" than they have had. They hope that their children will secure white-collar jobs. Most American parents believe that the best measure of their success in this life, and a good indication of their deserts in the future life, are to be found in the rise or fall of their children in the social scale.

The educational system bears these expectations as it operates in our social system. We shall see, now, how it meets these expectations.

The Educational System Is a Sorting and Selecting Agency

The educational system may be thought of as an enormous, complicated machine for sorting and ticketing and routing children through life. Young children are fed in at one end to a moving belt which conveys them past all sorts of inspecting stations. One large group is almost immediately brushed off into a bin labeled "nonreaders," "first-grade repeaters," or "opportunity class" where they stay for eight or ten years and are then released through a chute to the outside world to become "hewers of wood and drawers of water." The great body of children move ahead on the main belt, losing a few here and there who are "kept back" for repeated inspection.

At a station labeled "high school" there are several types of inspection and the main belt divides into smaller belts which diverge slightly from each other. From some of the belts the children, now become youths, are unceremoniously dumped down chutes into the outside world, while the other belts, labeled "college preparatory," "commercial," "vocational" roll steadily on. The young people are inspected not only for brains and learning ability, but also for skin color, pronunciation, cut of clothes, table manners, parental bank account. Strangely enough they are not inspected for moral integrity, honesty, or other qualities which go under the name of "character."

At the end of the high-school division several of the belts project their human freight into the outside labor market, and the sorting machine is now much smaller, housing a few narrow conveyors labeled "college," "professional school," and "trade school." The inspectors quickly shunt aside the majority of this small band of young men and women into the labor market, leaving a few indeed who reach the next station, labeled "bachelor's degree," which is the end of the machine really, though there is a small extension called "graduate school."

Whatever figure of speech we use, the school system appears to be a sorting device with various selective principles operating. In addition to the principle of intellectual ability, there are such principles of selection as economic status, social class, and social personality. There is little or no selection for moral character.

The Hometown school has already sorted out Tom Brown from Bob Jones. Tom will be promoted regularly and readied for college. Bob will be dropped as soon as possible. It is not yet clear what will happen to Joe Sienkowitz, but it appears that he will finish high school and because of his talent his teachers may help him to get a scholarship for study of music. There are probably two or three other boys in Tom Brown's class, fully as able as Tom, but without any special artistic talent, who will have to stop their education at the end of high school because their way into college is blocked by lack of money.

We can see how much selection takes place by looking at the figures for the numbers of young people who reach various levels of the educational ladder. Table I gives the number of youth out of a thousand who were reaching certain rungs of the ladder on two dates a generation apart, 1938 and 1910. The high school is much less selective at present than it was a generation ago. The college has also lost some of its selective quality though it remains a highly selective institution.

Through its function as a sorting agency the educational system is supposed to sift out the people with best brains and ability and to help them rise to the top. Thus the school is not only a system of education, it is also a system of elections. In America

TABLE I

THE SCHOOL AS A SELECTING AGENCY[1]

Number of People out of Every Thousand Who Reach a Given Educational Level

Level	1938	1910
First year high school (age 14)	850	310
Third year high school (age 16)	580	140
Graduation from high school (age 18)	450	93
Entrance to college or a similar educational institution	150	67
Graduation from college (Bachelor's degree)	70	23
Master's degree	9	1.5
Doctor of philosophy	1.3	

this system of elections is not 100 per cent efficient. That is, it does not succeed in selecting all the people with the best brains and ability and helping them to rise in the status system.

Educational Opportunity Is Not Equally Available to All

There are two senses in which we might say that educational opportunity is equally available to all children. We could speak of equal educational opportunity if all children and young people went to schools of their own choosing as long as they or their parents pleased. In that sense we fall far short of providing equal educational opportunity and we shall probably never attain such a goal.

In a more limited sense we might speak of equality of educational opportunity if all children and young people exceeding a given level of intellectual ability were enabled to attend schools and colleges up to some specified level. This is the only practicable kind of equality of educational opportunity. For example, if all boys and girls with I.Q.'s over 100 were able to attend high school up to the age of eighteen, and if all young people with I.Q.'s over 110 were able to attend college for four years, we could say that equality of educational opportunity existed to a considerable degree.

It is possible to investigate the availability of educational opportunity in this sense in various parts of the country. For example, a study of youth in Pennsylvania was conducted about a decade ago by the State Department of Public Instruction and the American Youth Commission.[2] The socio-economic status[3] and educational history were ascertained for a group of 910 pupils with intelligence quotients of 110 or above. It is generally assumed that pupils with intelligence quotients above 110 are good college material. This group of superior pupils was divided into two subgroups on the basis of socio-economic status. Of the upper socio-economic group, 93 per cent graduated from high school and 57 per cent attended college. Of the lower socio-economic group, 72 per cent graduated from high school and 13 per cent attended college. Further study of the data in Table II will show even more clearly that the group with below-average socio-economic status had relatively less educational opportunity than the group with above-average socio-economic status, although both groups were about equal in intellectual ability.

TABLE II

RELATION OF INTELLIGENCE TO EDUCATIONAL OPPORTUNITY

(Record of Students With Intelligence Quotients of 110 or Above)

Educational Advance	Socio-economic Status Above Average		Socio-economic Status Below Average		Total Group	
	No.	Per Cent	No.	Per Cent	No.	Per Cent
Dropped school at eighth grade or below	4	0.7	27	7.9	31	3.4
Completed ninth, tenth, or eleventh grade but did not graduate from high school	36	6.2	69	20.2	105	11.6
Graduated from high school but did not attend college	206	36.3	202	59.0	408	44.8
Attended college	322	56.8	44	12.9	366	40.2
Total	568	100.0	342	100.0	910	100.0

A similar conclusion must be drawn from a study made by Helen B. Goetsch[4] on 1,023 able students who graduated from Milwaukee high schools in 1937 and 1938. These students all had I.Q.'s of 117 or above. The income of their parents is directly related to college attendance, as is shown in Table III. The higher the parents' income, the greater is the proportion who went to college.

The same general result is found in the data of the National

TABLE III

RELATION OF PARENTAL INCOME TO FULL-TIME COLLEGE ATTENDANCE OF
SUPERIOR MILWAUKEE HIGH SCHOOL GRADUATES

Parental Income	Per Cent In College Full-time
$8,000+	100.0
5,000-7,999	92.0
3,000-4,999	72.9
2,000-2,999	44.4
1,500-1,999	28.9
1,000-1,499	25.5
500- 999	26.8
Under 500	20.4

Health Survey, which was conducted in eighty-three cities in eighteen states during the winter of 1935-36. When boys and girls of ages sixteen to twenty-four are classified by family income, school attendance increases markedly with increase in family income.[5]

It might be argued, in the face of these facts, that children of families in the lower socio-economic levels do not desire as much education as those from the middle and upper levels. Thus, if public grants were available to pay the living expenses of all high-school pupils who wished to go to school and needed financial help, we might still find that more children of the upper economic levels were attending school. But there are three lines of evidence which indicate that children at the lower economic levels do not have all the educational opportunity they or their parents desire. One is the frequency with which "lack of money" is given as a reason for quitting school.[6] Another is the sharp increase in college and high-school enrollment that came with the establishing of the National Youth Administration student-aid program in 1935. A third is the fact that there is a substantial out-of-pocket cost attached to attendance at a "free" high school. Hand has summarized a number of studies on the cash cost of going to a public high school. He finds this to average $125 a year in several cities.[7] Students can go to school and spend little or no money. But they are then barred from many of the school activities, they cannot even take regular laboratory courses, and they must go around in what is to high-school youngsters the supremely embarrassing condition of having no change to rattle in their pockets, no money to contribute to a party, no possibility of being independent in their dealings with their friends.

THE SOCIAL FUNCTIONS OF THE AMERICAN EDUCATIONAL SYSTEM

In the next chapter we shall see how different kinds of schools and different curricula within the schools are adapted to different social groups. Schools which are selective agencies, schools with different curricula for students with different expectations in life, must try to meet the expectations of many millions of American parents who want *their* children to have the kind of education which will promote them on the social ladder. It is impossible for the schools to meet all these expectations for all or even a majority of parents. Too many parents expect the impossible. They are too much interested in one of the functions of the school and perhaps not enough aware of other essential social functions which the school system performs in our society. The essential functions of the school system may be summarized under five heads.

1. To provide a basis of communication and a common core of traditions and values

In a going society, people must talk the same language, figuratively if not literally. They must read, write, and speak words which everybody understands, make change in a common currency, know and follow the same traffic rules. More than this, people must have common values, symbolized in common literature and tradition. They must have common heroes and common ideals, celebrated in well-known songs, stories, and pictures. On such occasions as a Fourth of July or Memorial Day celebration, an American Legion banquet, or a World Series baseball game, Americans of all classes must be able to get together and feel that they have things in common.

The elementary school provides this basis of common knowledge and common feeling. It teaches the three R's and it also teaches about Washington and Lincoln. Everybody learns to thrill at the words: "Give me liberty or give me death." It teaches "The Star-Spangled Banner" and "America, the Beautiful." Always through precept and sometimes through practice, it teaches the virtues of thrift, initiative, and ambition.

Tom Brown and Bob Jones and Joe Sienkowitz are learning these things in common. Kenneth Peabody is studying much the same things in his private school, but he is not learning them with other Hometown boys and he will always feel uncomfortable at affairs where he must adapt himself to people of all social classes. He will avoid these affairs, or attend them with mixed emotions. Tom Brown, on the other hand, will get a thrill out of such affairs when he becomes a man, and will revive in himself a feeling of comradeship on such occasions with Bob Jones and Joe Sienkowitz, who have grown up to occupy different social stations in life.

Recently the secondary school has taken on this same function, since it has become a school for nearly everybody. Consequently, we find a strong movement to "teach democracy" in the high school. The secondary school seeks to raise the common level of communication so that more complicated and more subtle things can be generally understood. This appears to be necessary so that men shall be able to solve the increasingly complex problems of modern society.

2. *To teach children to work and live together*

Young children are largely asocial. They have yet to learn the give-and-take, the co-operation and competition of adult social life. The family alone cannot teach them this. The school is an intermediate society between the family and the state which serves to train children in the ways of adult social life. In school and in play groups, which are a counterpart of school, they learn the why and wherefore of moral rules and they come to terms with social authority in the form of rules and laws made by the adult society.

3. *To help people find ways of realizing their social ideals*

Education, and particularly higher education, is to some extent the teacher of society. A changing society needs a continually renewed supply of technological knowledge and ethical insight to solve its problems of living. The colleges and universities, and to a lesser degree the high schools, are places where people explore and discover the truth that is needed to improve their society. Thus education is not restricted to the task of adjusting people to the present social order. It also has the task of preparing people to change and improve the social order.

4. To teach the skills for carrying on the economic life of society

In a society whose economic life depends upon a division of labor among its members into a variety of jobs, many of which require a considerable degree of special knowledge and skill, the educational system must help people to secure this special knowledge and skill. The responsibility rests mainly upon the secondary school and the college.

The secondary school teaches agriculture, homemaking, bookkeeping, stenography, automobile repairing, simple industrial arts, commercial art, printing, and the basic reading and calculating skills necessary for a college course leading to such professions as medicine, engineering, chemistry, and teaching.

The junior college in its terminal courses teaches skills which are more complicated than those taught in high school, as indicated by the term "semiprofessional" which describes these courses. The junior college prepares medical and dental assistants, radio repair men, secretaries, bank clerks, photographers, laboratory and shop technicians, and certain kinds of civil servants.

The college and the professional school teach the more demanding skills, such as those involved in engineering, medicine, dentistry, chemistry, law, social work, ministry, and business administration.

This function of the educational system is related to the status system through the fact that economic skill and social status are usually closely correlated up to the level of upper-middle class status. The higher one goes in the educational hierarchy, the higher will his economic status probably become and the higher will his social status probably become (up to the upper-middle level). Furthermore, the higher the economic and social status of one's family (up to the upper-middle level), the higher one goes in the educational hierarchy.

5. To select and train children for social mobility

Most children are trained by home and neighborhood to occupy the social positions to which they are born. The school offers some opposition to home and neighborhood training in the case of the lower-class children but usually fights a losing battle over them. It supports and supplements the home and neighborhood training of middle-class children. It tends to democratize the training of upper-class children but loses many of these children to private schools which give them a class education.

While the school has relatively little influence on the training for social position of a majority of children, it does have a significant effect on a significant minority of children. The school system selects many children of lower- and middle-class status and helps them to rise in the social and economic scales. It performs this function by giving these children an opportunity to:

Associate with children of middle and upper social status.
Learn the social skills of middle and upper status.
Learn the vocational skills of middle and upper economic status.

This is mainly a function of high school and college.

To understand the selective nature of the American educational system it is necessary to keep in mind the fact that this selectivity has two aspects. First, the school system serves the children of different classes in different ways; and second, the school system selects a minority and trains them for social mobility. The one aspect of selectivity operates to preserve the status system, and the other aspect operates to help some children secure the reward of climbing within the status system.

These are the social functions of the educational system. Most parents see them only dimly and partially. The educator must see them clearly and bear them all in mind as he goes about his business. He must also bear in mind the fact that the function of promoting social mobility is the one that is best understood and valued most highly by parents.

CHAPTER V

Curricula—Selective Pathways to Success

CLASS AND CURRICULA

IN WHAT ways does the school contribute to the American status system? How does the school function in this status system? These are the problems we are here investigating. First, let us look at what is taught in school against the background of the American status system. In the technical language of school personnel, "what is taught" in school is described as "the curriculum." In many high schools throughout the country there are different curricula or courses leading to different kinds of diplomas and to different walks of life. In some large communities we find that there are different schools for these different courses, such as manual training school, vocational school, commercial school, technical school, trade school, and so on. Not all communities can afford such elaborate programs, but we find variations from the extremes of many courses and schools to schools with one generalized curriculum.

Who takes what curriculum in high school? How is the choice made? Such are the questions we must ask and answer. We might first look at a high school where there are no formal differences of curriculum but where elective courses differentiate the college preparatory from other students. The school superintendent of Old City, in talking about the school's role in the choice of courses, says:

I try not to encourage them all to go to college but neither do I try to discourage them. I do feel that it is much better that those who will not make good college material do not go to college and I try to impress on them that there is no magic in college and that those who make good there would probably make good anyway. I also must keep in mind the fact that if our students go to college and make a poor record it reflects on us and hurts our standing and for that reason I try to discourage the poorer students from going to college. Another thing that must be kept in mind is that the students who go to college seldom return here and the students who are

58

going to make good citizens and taxpayers ten years from now are those who are not of exceptional ability and are not college material.

He states further at another time:

> I have noticed that although a student must have at least medium ability to enter college, the way the courses are given he may go through and get a degree and all he will have will be an assortment of courses such as impractical psychology, sociology, economics, and things like that which I admit are good things but with the average student don't prepare him for actual life. The result is that a boy who might have made a good brick-mason comes out with a smattering of useless knowledge and a feeling that brick work is beneath him and he just struggles along with some work he is not fitted for. You know, when I was a boy, the professors and teachers used to tell us that we should be ambitious and that if we were and worked hard each of us might get to be president. As a result we had these big ideas and struggled for something that we might have known we couldn't get. I don't believe in that and so I try to tell them that it is better to be a farmer and have a comfortable and happy life than try to be something you are not fitted for.

We see what actually happens if we consider the 191 students who were graduates of the Old City High School over a five-year period. This number includes all the white high-school graduates except those who attended private schools. Table IV shows

TABLE IV

COLLEGE ATTENDANCE OF HIGH SCHOOL GRADUATES IN OLD CITY

Class	Number	% of Total by Class	Number Attending College	% of Each Social Class Attending College	% by Social Class of All Who Attend College
Upper	14	7	10	72	14
Upper middle	54	28	37	69	51
Middle	31	16	18	58	25
Lower middle	43	23	7	16	10
Lower	19	10	0	0	0
Unknown	30	16	0	0	0
Total	191	100	72		100

what happened to these people after graduation and what the social make-up of the group was.

The group called "middle" is made up of those about whom not enough is known to stratify exactly so that it consists of both upper-middle and lower-middle class people. The group called "lower" is made up of all upper-lower and lower-lower class people. The group marked "unknown" were those about whom there was insufficient information for classification, but for the most part these came from the rural areas or from a near-by orphanage.

We must note that most of the upper-class students attend college but that they form only 7 per cent of the total graduating class. The upper-middle class students make up 28 per cent of the graduating class and 69 per cent of them go on to college, whereas the lower-middle class makes up 23 per cent of the graduating class and only 16 per cent of them go on to college. Stated another way, of all those who go on to college, the upper-class students constitute 14 per cent, and there are no lower-class students during this period who go on to college.

One boy, the son of an immigrant truck farmer of lower-middle class status, won a national essay contest and will go to college on a scholarship and probably will rise in status. Another lower-middle class boy who did not have much scholastic ability but who was an excellent football player went on to college and one can predict upward mobility for him because he also has an affable personality. Two lower-middle class sisters who are talented musicians continued their musical training after high school and at the time of the study had already begun to participate freely, albeit as artists, with upper-middle and upper-class people.

There are four curricula in the Yankee City high school. The Latin course, including modern and classical languages as well as history and mathematics, is designed to prepare students for college. The scientific course emphasizes physics and chemistry and prepares the student for college study, but it does not equip him to get a job in an applied science. The commercial course, with such subjects as typewriting, shorthand, and commercial English, is supposed to train the pupil so that he can get a job when he leaves high school. The general course provides a high-school pupil with an adequate education for immediate adjustment to life. To reiterate, the first two courses provide preparation for college and the last two for immediate acceptance of adult status. A "D" mark is not passing in Latin or scientific curricula but it is passing in general or commercial. This is indication of the scholastic difference between the Latin and scientific and the general and commercial curricula.

All the pupils from the upper-upper class went to private

schools which prepared for college. All the lower-upper pupils in the public high school were in the scientific or the Latin course. Eighty-eight per cent of the upper-middle class, 45 per cent of the lower-middle class, only 28 per cent of the upper-lower, and 26 per cent of the lower-lower took college-preparatory work. As the social class declines, there is a progressive drop in the percentage of the pupils who take courses to prepare them for college, and there is a progressive increase in the percentage of pupils who take the commercial and the general courses. Only 12 per cent of the upper-middle class pupils took the commercial and the general courses, compared with 55 per cent of the lower-middle class, 72 per cent of the upper-lower, and 74 per cent of the lower-lower.

The evidence is clear that the class system of Yankee City definitely exercises a control over the pupils' choices of curricula. Supplementary interviewing of teachers and principals abundantly demonstrated this point. The children of the two upper and the upper-middle classes, in overwhelming percentages, were learning and being taught a way of life which would fit them into higher statuses. On the other hand, the lower-middle and the lower-class children, in their studies in the high school, were learning a way of life which would help adjust them to the rank in which they were born.

In the elementary school all the children from all the classes are given the same formal training. In high school social differentiation begins. The formal education of the high school itself clearly contributes to the social differences which begin to appear in the personalities of the children. Nevertheless, a certain percentage of the lower-class children in high school do take the preparatory course for college. Those who do are usually socially mobile and are using the high school to equip themselves for climbing to a higher rung on the social ladder. They are said by their teachers to be "more ambitious" than the others.

The class differences in choice of high-school course show up in other interesting ways. The principal, for instance, says that the standard of teaching lowers as one goes from Latin to general course. He says:

In the past the teaching was different in the Latin group from the scientific group, but now they are both to be the same. There was a recognizable difference in the quality of teaching formerly so that you weren't able to shift one pupil from the scientific to the Latin curriculum, although you could shift him from the Latin to the scientific. Next year there will more than ever be a difference in the college and noncollege group. It is like having two schools within one building. This difference exists in English as a subject, but also in the other studies. For example, take the General Science Course III and the Chemistry course given in the scientific curriculum. The latter is more difficult and includes more material and is better taught than the former.

This teaching difference is not particularly perceptible to the students. According to one bright boy from the upper-lower class:

The Latin curriculum only means that Latin is inserted in that curriculum Even if you don't go to college the Latin curriculum does you some good. I wish that I had taken the commercial course because now I expect to study advertising in some school in Boston. When I entered high school, I thought I might go on to college, but I can't now. I wish though we didn't have to study French. If I flunk French, I might have to graduate in the general curriculum. That would be too bad.

Even though this boy does not believe there is much difference in the courses he knows the social value of graduating in the Latin curriculum. In discussing school activities, this same boy says:

On the school magazine staff there are more from the Latin division than from any of the others, that is, three Latin students, two general, two commercial and two scientific.

Three Latin division students are active editors on the yearbook, all, that is, except for the business manager, who is from the scientific division.

We find further that the people in these various curricula stick together and vie for social recognition. For instance, we hear a boy discussing the school leaders.

Kathleen Regan is vice-president of the Student Council, and is very popular with her classmates. She belongs to the Tri-Hi Club, is on the magazine staff, was a class officer in a previous year, and had a leading part in the cast of the senior play. Whenever there is any party, Tri-Hi dances, etc., around, John Burton usually takes Kathleen. She is a darn good kid; she has been in my class four years now, in the Latin division. You know the friendships one makes in school last for a long time.

Then there is Ruth Larkin, president of the English Club, in the Latin division, and on the Student Council as a result of being president of the English Club.

And William Carlyle, auditor of his year, business manager of the yearbook, member of Hi-Y, editor-in-chief of the magazine, has held class offices, doesn't go around with any special kids, and in school doesn't hang around with anybody in particular. He wouldn't be getting the recognition that he is if it wasn't for his friends in the scientific division, who elected him to his office. This is common in the case of quiet kids. He is an honor student.

The intellectual talent of these children is being trained and prepared for upward mobility. They are now feeling the effect of this combination of curriculum and talent in their increase in status.

Social class shows its influence more directly in these school activities. About Mike Ryan, an upper-lower class boy, we are told that he is

a popular little Riverbrooker. He was elected president of the sophomore class by a margin of three or four votes. The election was between him and Edwin Hatley from up the Hill. The election was really between the River-brookers and the Hill, and it took three or four ballots to reach the decision. Finally, Ryan won by six votes. Both these kids are very friendly with each other. The kids were voting for the one that came from their section of the city.

In athletics, however, this accent on social background and future plans (college) are not important or may be in fact reversed.

Peter, our rugged football star, comes from the tough section of the city, where they think a lot of the football players that come from there. He chums around with Eddy. They are both to be captains of the football team next year. Their parents work in shoe factories. Eddy's father died suddenly last year. Had a heart attack before the football season. The family is struggling along. They have always been poor. An older brother, Sydney, probably is the only means of support now. The mother naturally stays at home because they have small children.

Gordon Warren is a redheaded football player called "the carrot-topped demon." The fellows are always laughing when he is around. He does a lot of dancing and has a swagger all his own on the dance floor. The girls all like him as he has a very likable character; he is a jolly kid, has freckles, red hair, and has a glass eye. He comes from the South End.

In discussing another boy from the lower-lower class, our informant shows how differentiation is present and how by being good enough in schoolwork and doing the right thing one can get in with the "higher-ups" and if "the friendship is lasting" one can "really get ahead."

Now, there is Mike, an active member of the Student Council, treasurer of the senior class, and treasurer of the Student Council. He comes from the poorer section of the city. He is in the Latin course and will probably win a scholarship. He is very well liked by those that know him in the school. He plays football, baseball, and doesn't go around with any girl, doesn't show any inclination for stepping out. When the Hi-Y club puts on a party or social, Mike doesn't seem to have any trouble getting a girl, so I guess he's all right. His parents are pretty poor, I imagine, but that doesn't hold against him. I think just as much of him as I do of the kids up the Hill. In fact, more. The kids from the Hill are from a richer class. You don't have to come from the Hill to be in that group, but they usually stick together—they usually have a clique of their own. I don't know whether they think they're better than other kids, although maybe the poorer kids think they are snobs. My class is pretty free from that. Those that stick together are usually well liked. Most of these kids are very well liked by kids from the other division.

How the Students Make Their Selection of Curricula

As we have seen, the social class status of a pupil and his family has considerable influence in the choice of high-school curriculum so that lower-upper, upper-middle, and lower-middle class children go in strongly for the college preparatory course and the others tend to choose the more vocational courses. This tendency of social class standards to overrule ability leads to a good deal of reshuffling or attempted reshuffling by the high-school teachers. That is, they have to try to change some of the good students from the vocational courses to the college preparatory courses and, by giving failing marks, they change students from Latin or science to the general course.

If the pupil is intent on getting ahead and does not have the characteristics which the teacher thinks are necessary, he is dissuaded from pinning his hopes too high. If the student, on the other hand, is not confident enough in his ability to get ahead but the teacher recognizes this ability, it is the teacher's responsibility to start him on the right path.

A woman teacher in the high school says:

Children in the grammar school make very silly decisions. Two of the four girls who are highest in the senior class this year elected commercial or general their freshman year, and shifted to Latin at the end of the freshman year; but neither one can graduate in Latin because they haven't had the first year of Latin. If they had been guided to make the correct decision earlier they would have been able to graduate in the Latin curriculum.

The high-school principal generalizes about the changes from the college preparatory courses:

The changes made by the pupils from a Latin or scientific curriculum to the commercial or general were usually forced, that is, a pupil should never have been there. Such things as failure to do the work properly force a pupil to change in order to be able to graduate. It is a tragedy, the large

number who are taking Latin or scientific curricula who shouldn't really
be there. They come to high school with some idea that they ought to
prepare for college whether they have the ability or not.

Note the idea of place, that is, a pupil in the Latin or scientific
is "there," he isn't just taking a special course.

The condition of the high-school equipment and building is an
example of the influence of the social class system on the schools.
No upper-uppers and a small portion of the lower-uppers send
their children to the local school. These people, by controlling the
banks and large industries, control the financing of the city; and,
although the school has been inadequate on all scores for thirty
years, no money has been allotted to build a new school.

A new school was important for the upper-middle class who
based their hopes for "getting ahead" on education. It was the
City Council that controlled the funds, however, and they knew
who controlled the town. The City Council frustrated the efforts
of the upper-middle class Board of Education to get a new school.
A high-school boy says:

> I showed the school board all through the school building the other day,
> and showed them all the sore spots. The school board is all for having a new
> building. A City Council committee, including the mayor, also visited the
> school and this committee thought that only the laboratory was inadequate
> and thought that it was foolish to have such a little room way up on the
> top floor for a laboratory.

The history of educational institutions in Yankee City goes a
long way back into the eighteenth century. Since the beginning,
Yankee City set up grammar schools in which the three R's were
taught. In 1831 a high school was begun for boys. In 1843 a high
school for girls was begun, and in 1844 a free school for boys and
girls was opened. All those schools were privately endowed, and
they were the basis of the Yankee City high school, which was
started in 1868 as an amalgamation of the other three schools. The
purpose of the three schools was to prepare the boys for college
and the professions and the girls for teaching, as well as to give
them subjects which were "solid and useful." Only "the better
class" of young person went on to secondary education. As the
demand for educated people grew in the United States and high
schools expanded, the Yankee City High School was adapted to
the changing situation. This was done by adding vocational and
commercial courses to the Latin and scientific courses. The school
board, however, steadfastly refused to increase the building

accommodation, so that in 1932 the high school, planned to seat 350 students, was squeezing in 800.

Who Prepares for College in Hometown

The Hometown school has a fine building and an undifferentiated curriculum so that the same high-school education is available to all the children, whether they have college ambitions or not. In Hometown, 80 per cent of the boys and girls of high-school age attend high school. Why do they go? What do they and their parents expect from a high-school education?

First of all, no upper-upper class family has children in high school. The lower-uppers and upper-middles account for about the same proportions of pupils as one would expect from their proportions in the total population. The lower-middles contribute less than one would expect and the upper-lower and lower-lower contribute more, probably because the lower-class people have larger families and, therefore, more prospective pupils.

Of all high-school students classified as lower-upper or upper-middle, 88 per cent will go on to college while only 12 per cent of those in the three bottom classes expect to go to college. Of the total high-school pupils, 20 per cent are preparing to go to college and 80 per cent were definitely not going to college.

TABLE V

College Expectations and Social Position

Proportion of High-School Students Expecting to Go to College

Class	Hometown	Yankee City
	Per Cent	Per Cent
Upper upper		
Lower upper	100	100
Upper middle	80	88
Lower middle	22	45
Upper lower	9	28
Lower lower	0	26

In Table V we can see how the college expectations of high-school students compare with their social class positions. College expectations in Hometown were determined largely on the basis of the high-school principal's judgment concerning the probability of college attendance for each individual student. Combined with this was a consideration of the emphasis placed on strictly academic work and the stated expectations of the students about going on to college. It is important to notice that the greater proportion or all the upper-middle and lower-upper classes will go on to college while only a small proportion or none at all of the three lower groups expect to go to college. When we look at college expectations of Yankee City youth, we see a somewhat similar picture. Proportionately more lower-middle and lower-class students in Yankee City are thinking in terms of college, but this derives from the fact that in Yankee City there is a fund which helps boys to go through college and also from the fact that a smaller proportion of lower-class students are in high school. College expectation of Yankee City students is derived from figures on curriculum choice.

Very few Hometown boys and girls have gone away to private preparatory schools. People of the higher strata were unanimous in saying, "It's not done in Hometown."

Mr. Peabody sends his son, Kenneth, to one of the famous New England "prep" schools. He says, "I can see a difference," and such invidious comparisons annoy some people in Hometown. In Yankee City almost all upper-upper children and many lower-upper and some upper-middle children are sent to private schools.

In Hometown, adults of any given class seem to vary considerably with respect to the education they have had, and this seems to be the more true in the higher strata. There are men in the higher strata who are not high-school graduates and some who are graduates of professional schools having considerable prestige; and there have been college men on WPA along with adults who have attended less than seven grades of grammar school.

As a rule, the adults in any given class expect their children to receive the "same" or "better" education than they themselves received, and their primary evaluation of "education" is in terms of quantity; they think in terms of "how many grades" or "how many years" of high school or college. When they evaluate the "quality" of education, they use either or both of two kinds of rough measures: first, the measures of pupil performance (marking system, graduation honors, etc.) and, second, the social prestige of the school involved.

How does the high school fulfill the expectations of the people of Hometown? The curriculum is to a large extent built around requirements for college entrance, and for the 20 per cent of the students who continue their education in institutions of higher learning the preparation is adequate, if judged by the subsequent academic achievement of Hometown students at colleges. This college preparatory group is preponderantly upper-middle and lower-middle class, with a few lower-uppers and upper-lowers.

Other students in the high school take mostly courses in the college preparatory curriculum with some vocational subjects instead of Latin, modern languages, and mathematics. There are agricultural courses, business and secretarial courses, and an apprenticeship program by which students are trained as clerks in the stores or as workmen in the factories.

For the children of high-status families "life begins in college," for the high school no longer provides the class training people of these positions have so long expected of it. "Life begins in high school" for the lower-middle and lower classes. Hometown people feel that they are very "democratic" and do not like to be at all reminded of their stratified status system. It is up to Mr. Mercer, the school principal, to provide a high-school curriculum and learning system that fulfills the requirements of all without too noticeable differentiation. Also, he has to do this in a way that will not offend his school board, which consists of three upper-middle class men and two lower-uppers. Here is what Mr. Mercer says:

> What I'm interested in is the curriculum in the wider sense—that includes the school orchestra, dances for young people, and things like that. Curriculum in the narrow sense is the traditional thing; parents want their kids to have the same things they did. You can't change this, you can't change the curriculum in the narrow sense—I know you can change these other things [the extracurricular activities] but you can't change the traditional curriculum.

So Andrew Mercer steers his way between the extremes of an education suited, on the one hand, to the majority and, on the other hand, to the most powerful. His success is shown in that he has come up from a lowly position—country boy "with no poise" —to be an accepted member of the upper-middle class. Even Judge Scott, one of the town's most successful social arbiters, finds him a fine fellow—"got what it takes," he says.

The attitude of "getting ahead" pervades the whole of Home-town and there is "democratic" social atmosphere reminiscent of the late nineteenth century. The bulk of the population (91 per cent) is lower-middle and lower class; and there still seems to be room "at the top." We see examples of this attitude in action in the Rotary Club program to Americanize the lower-class ethnic population. At a Rotary dinner for the Polish boys' baseball team the team captain said that all the boys hoped to grow up to belong to Rotary (a middle-class organization). The school fits into and adds to this attitude toward upward mobility. This is best exemplified in the reaction against a differentiated curriculum in the high school. The democratic way seems to be to give everyone the same educational opportunities—the same as required for those at the top, namely, college preparatory courses.

The school system of Hometown, especially the high school, reflects the democratic belief that everyone has a chance to "get to the top." In other words, the democratic ideal of "opportunity for all" is a guiding principle and the school is the main instrument of opportunity. It performs this function, as the schools did more generally a generation or two ago in America, by offering an undifferentiated general academic education; he can take this opportunity who will.

It is clear now that Kenneth Peabody and Tom Brown will go to college, like nearly everyone else at their status level. They will have social pressure applied to them to push ahead. Joe Sienkowitz and his brother come from a class where few go on to college, but Joe with his musical ability and his brother with athletic talent will rise in the status system because they will translate the power given them by their talent into social recognition. Bob Jones and his kind are destined to populate the lower levels of our social system.

SOME HIGH SCHOOLS PROVIDE A SINGLE PROGRAM
FOR YOUTH OF ALL STATUSES

In certain large cities, the undifferentiated high school, which we have seen in Hometown, is in general favor, even though the schools are large enough to permit differentiation.

One of the more significant social experiments of our time is being carried on in a number of city high schools in the Middle West and West. In Denver, Tulsa, Des Moines, Phoenix, Los Angeles, Oakland, and other cities like them, the high schools are nearly all of the "comprehensive" type. All students are in a single curriculum, with many individual electives, but without hard and fast divisions into college preparatory, commercial, vocational, etc. Thus there are no divisions on the basis of which claims to social status can be made. All kinds of students are in the same English, mathematics, and history courses, regardless of their college-going intentions. Some students elect commercial or other "vocational" subjects in preference to "college preparatory" subjects, but they are not set off as a separate group of students with a separate curriculum. This situation holds also for most of the small cities like Hometown where the enrollment is too small to permit much differentiation of curricula.

The schools in these cities are criticized by many upper-middle class people because they do not have "high standards" and do not "prepare well for college." Yet a comprehensive and careful study of the college records of students from several of these schools shows that in college they do as well as or better than do the graduates from traditional college-preparatory curricula and traditional high schools with a college-preparatory emphasis.[1]

It is probable that the criticisms coming from upper-middle class people come in part from uneasiness over the threatened disintegration of social-status lines in the high school with the disappearance of clearly marked differences among curricula. On the other hand, these schools are praised by many educators for the contributions they make to democratic citizenship and to helping boys and girls achieve the task of growing up in a complex society. It may be suspected that these high schools draw a good deal of their popular support from lower-middle and lower-class parents who want their children to have "all the advantages of education," and do not like the discrimination implied by differentiation of curricula.

A FEW HIGH SCHOOLS SERVE YOUTH OF A SINGLE STATUS

In sharp contrast to the cosmopolitan high school serving youth of all statuses is the high school of certain metropolitan suburbs, which draws students from a narrow segment of society. In such suburbs as Bronxville and Manhasset (New York City), Winnetka and Lake Forest (Chicago), Grosse Pointe (Detroit), and Shaker Heights (Cleveland), the population is preponderantly upper-middle class, and the high school is remarkably homogeneous as to social status. Of course, there are many graduations of status in a suburb of this type, but these are mainly subdivisions of a national upper-middle class. While the teachers in these communities point with pride to their one or two Negro or Chinese students and to the children of chauffeurs, cooks, and grocerymen, the fact is that youngsters like these, who make up the backbone of the public-school population of the ordinary town, are a conspicuous minority in the upper-middle class suburb. Thus, in such a community, the school is largely a one-status institution.

COLLEGES ALSO FIT THE STATUS SYSTEM

At the college level there is a variety of institutions corresponding roughly to social differences in college students as well as to their differences in vocational goals.

Teachers' colleges and normal schools draw their students largely from lower-middle and upper-lower class families.[2] Tom Brown's teacher, Virginia Crane, attended normal school and graduated from a teachers' college.

Junior colleges are so varied in type that no single generalization can be made concerning them. The municipal junior colleges, such as the Chicago City Junior Colleges, tend to draw students from lower-middle and lower classes. Some private junior colleges, especially those for girls, draw largely from the upper-middle class, giving their students a training closely adapted to the social and vocational life of that class. Stephens College is an example of this group.

The state and municipal universities come nearest to getting a cross section of young people. However, the bulk of their students are from upper-middle and lower-middle class families. For example, the University of California at Berkeley draws heavily from middle-class families in the San Francisco Bay region, while many boys and girls from upper-class families go to Stanford.[3]

The church-related college and the independent liberal arts college of the South, Middle West, and West also draw from upper-middle and lower-middle class families, though with significant differences due to the predominance of liberal arts or of religious emphasis in their programs. Oberlin, Carleton, Beloit, Knox, Ohio Wesleyan, DePauw, Pomona, Whitman, Davidson, and Mercer are citadels of the middle class.

The old-established eastern colleges and universities draw from the upper-middle and upper classes, with a sprinkling of mobile lower-middle class youth. These are the "Ivy League" institutions —Yale, Harvard, Princeton, Dartmouth, Amherst, Williams,

Hamilton, Haverford, etc. Like them are a few colleges and universities west of the Alleghenies, of which Stanford is the outstanding example.

The generalization that different curricula and types of institutions are adapted to different statuses is illustrated by Goetsch's study.[4] She found that the hierarchy of family income was reflected in a hierarchy of courses pursued by students in higher institutions, as shown in Table VI.

TABLE VI

PARENTAL INCOME AND COLLEGE COURSES

Curriculum	Median Parental Income
Law	$2,118
Medicine and Dentistry	2,112
Liberal Arts	2,068
Journalism	1,907
Engineering	1,884
Teaching	1,570
Commercial	1,543
Nursing	1,368
Industrial Trades	1,104

In each of these groups of institutions we see that the program is adapted to boys and girls from a certain portion of the social range. But equally significant is the fact that in nearly all these schools and colleges there is a substantial minority from lower positions in the social heap who are achieving social mobility through their education.

CHAPTER VI

Status in the Classroom

CLASS AND THE RATING OF A CHILD'S ABILITY

WE HAVE tried to show how the academic offerings of the school are related to social status. Other factors in the school may also be related to social status. Children are put in the proper grades, the grades are sectioned, there are preferential seating arrangements, there are different buildings for different areas. Children gain or lose status, too, depending on their teachers. Is the social status of a child's family in any way related to these status-giving factors? Or are all judgments made in school based on ability and achievement as is commonly believed?

Outwardly, the school is that institution which sorts out people by achievement, and as the standards of judgment seem to be fairly objective, we might believe that the school is not closely bound to the social structure in which it exists or that, if it is, then the social classes tend to separate out with those with the most intelligence at the top of the school and those with the least at the bottom.

In some elementary schools where there is more than one classroom per grade there is a section system by which students are rated and put together into A section, B section, C section, and more if necessary. In Old City, we find such a system. Each grade is divided into three sections: A, B, and C. This division into sections pervades the whole school system but of necessity it has less formal characteristics in the later years of high school. The junior high-school principal says of these sections:

> When a child enters school he is put into one of three sections according to what the teacher thinks his ability is. When you have dealt with children much you soon find that you can pretty well separate them into three groups according to ability. Then if a child shows more ability he may be shifted into a higher group or if he fails he may be moved into a lower group.

Sometime later when this same principal was asked whether there seemed to be any class distinctions between the sections, he answered:

There is to some extent. You generally find that children from the best families do the best work. That is not always true but usually it is so. The children from the lower class seem to be not as capable as the others. I think it is to some extent inheritance. The others come from people who are capable and educated, and also the environment probably has a great effect. They come to school with a lot of knowledge already that the others lack.

Whatever one may think of this principal's theory in explanation of the correlation between social position and school section, this correlation holds true. There is a strong relationship between social status and rank in school. An analysis of the classes of three years in which the social position of 103 girls was known, shows that

(1) of the ten upper-class girls eight were in section A, one in B, and one in C
(2) of the seven upper-middle class girls, six were in section A and one in B
(3) of the thirty-three girls from lower middle and indeterminate middle class, twenty-one were in section A, ten in section B, and two in section C
(4) of the fifty-three lower-class girls, only six were in section A, twenty-eight in section B, and nineteen in section C.

A teacher in junior high school was willing and able to talk more explicitly about these sections than was the principal quoted above. This teacher was asked if there was "much class feeling in the school" and she said:

Oh, yes, there is a lot of that. We try not to have it as much as we can but of course we can't help it. Now, for instance, even in the sections we have, it is evident. Sections are supposed to be made up just on the basis of records in school but it isn't and everybody knows it isn't. I know right in my own A section I have children who ought to be in B section, but they are little socialites and so they stay in A. I don't say there are children in B who should be in A but in the A section there are some who shouldn't be there. We have discussed it in faculty meetings but nothing is ever done.

Later on, she said:

Of course, we do some shifting around. There are some borderliners who were shifted up to make the sections more nearly even. But the socialites who aren't keeping up their standard in the A section were never taken into B or C section and they never will. They don't belong there socially. Of course, there are some girls in A section who don't belong there socially, but almost everyone of the socialites is in A.

In Old City the ranking of students in their classrooms is clearly influenced by status considerations.

The Dorland School

In the south end of Yankee City is the largest grammar school. This, the Dorland School, draws pupils from a largely lower-class area but there are some pupils from the higher classes with the exception of upper-upper. In the eighth grade, for instance, we find that of 112 pupils in one year there were four upper-middles, eleven lower-middles, twenty-eight upper-lowers, and forty-nine lower-lowers. In other words, over 80 per cent of the children in Dorland School are either upper-lower or lower-lower class. Not far away is Ashton School in a better-class neighborhood but there are still many lower-class children attending. In each of these two schools the section system prevails. Furthermore, Ashton School is considered to be of a higher intellectual level than Dorland. In case of those who live near the borderline of the school districts the assignment of the students by the school authorities is based more on class status than on ability. The superintendent says: "Hill Street children would only be held back if forced to be in the same group as the children of Riverbrookers. So there are three groups: Hill Streeters, intermediates, and Riverbrookers." There are then two kinds of grouping to be seen —different schools for different sections of the city and the section system of classrooms.

There is a difference of attitude of the school authorities toward these schools. Although Yankee City spent little money on its school equipment, proportionately less was expended for the schools in the poorer areas than for others. The Dorland School was in the greatest disrepair. An observer reports:

Greer [the principal] took me upstairs to show me the condition of the building. Sickly green walls, dirty and grimy. The upstairs room is an auditorium but obviously improvised. He said that here they were talking about unemployment and the school was drying for lack of paint. We then went down to the basement, where Greer wanted to show me the kind of thing that the municipal government allowed. In the first place, there was a large part of the basement which was unused, and he had wanted to put in a manual training department there. He has six classes who take manual training, which is about four more than all the rest of the city. If he sends his pupils up to the Ashton School, it takes twenty minutes up and twenty minutes back, which makes forty minutes out of the school day and amounts to two hours a week wasted. They told him the place was damp and poorly lit, both of which are untrue, since it is close to the furnace and lighted by large windows, but since the North End group have the power these were only alibis.

He then took me to the boiler room to show how inadequate the heating arrangement was. There are five small furnaces, two on each end and one in the middle each of which heats about two rooms. They are very wasteful and require constant attention and supply little heat. If the regular janitor, who is an able man, got sick and a strange man took charge, there would be a lot of trouble. The furnaces are full of holes which are patched up and if the damper was put a little too low the whole school would be full of coal gas in an hour. We went upstairs and he pointed out that the only lights were in the halls and that with no lights in the classrooms the children were ruining their eyesight, but with this, as with the furnaces, nothing was done. This was especially bad, since, as psychologists have shown, visualization is about 25 per cent more effective in learning processes than audition, and he hoped the time would come when they could teach by sight instead of audition, especially since our civilization is geared to visualization.

There can be no doubt that the powerful middle-class, by their influence on the schools, tend to contribute to the subordination of the lower classes by refusing equipment to schools which are predominantly lower class. The Dorland School is the only school without lighting in all of its classrooms.

Mr. Greer had to run the school and work out programs which fitted into the city school curriculum and with the background of the pupils. The first thing he did was to institute a "section system," by which the pupils were divided into three sections according to their ability. The ability of the child was judged by the teachers. The children were also given an intelligence test. The superintendent of schools once said that the A section was for Hill Streeters, B for the middle group, and C for the River-brookers. However, Greer, the principal, says:

That is the very thing it wasn't. If we had put in anything like that we couldn't have kept it for more than ten minutes. I have been very careful to explain to everyone that there is no division on social bases and that just as many children from the poorer classes are in the A groups as in the C groups.

When we first put the system in a good many parents came up to find out why their children were in the C group and I told them all it meant was that they were being taught the same material in a slightly different fashion and that they all would do the same work whether they were in the A, B, or C group. The kids had no feeling whatsoever about being in A, B, or C. There is no social grading connected with this system. Parents would have raised hell if there had been a Hill Streeter-Riverbrooker distinction.

However, when asked specifically whether the C group was from the lower economic levels he said most emphatically:

Yes, the A group is highest in that respect, but the B group includes in its extremes children who might belong to either A or C groups. The B group includes some characterized by the metaphysical concept of mental laziness,

They have the brains but they don't work hard. The B group also includes those who would be in the A group in a grade below but would flunk if put in the A group of the present grade. Finally, it includes hard workers from the C group.

Greer thinks that this A, B, C system prevents children from becoming misfits and keeps them from causing a lot of trouble. He gave one instance of a boy who was in the fifth grade and was not in the right group. "Since the work was beyond him all he did was raise hell. He was shifted into C section and now he is perfectly happy." He said it was ridiculous to think that the only bright children came from Hill Street. In the first place, the Hill Streeters have given up having children any more and he doesn't think there are many from Hill Street in the school. There are plenty of Riverbrookers who are bright; two of his brightest pupils, with the highest I.Q.'s in the school, are Riverbrookers. No one in this part of town has any idea that there is a distinction on the basis of Hill Street and Riverbrook. They all understand that the children are getting the same work.

Mr. Greer is certain that (a) the children are ranked in the sections on the basis of ability and (b) higher-class children are generally more able than lower-class children, so that there really is Hill Streeter-Riverbrooker difference. He means that the judgment of ability is primarily a social class judgment and those children who conform to middle-class standards have ability.

If we look at Table VII, we can see how this judgment operates in the eighth grade.

TABLE VII

EIGHTH GRADE—DORLAND SCHOOL

(Distribution in Sections by Social Class)

Section	A Per Cent	B Per Cent	C Per Cent
Upper middle	12	0	0
Lower middle	12	14	9
Upper lower	44	36	0
Lower lower	32	50	91
	100	100	100

The sample is not large enough to make any distinct differentiations but the facts that the upper-middle class students are all in

Section A and that Section C is so predominantly lower-lower class are significant in showing that the lower-class children do not tend to participate with those above lower-middle.

The teachers show their feeling that the sections are status groups. Greer, in talking about the A, B, C arrangement, said:

The teachers were dreadfully upset when they knew that this was going on, worrying for fear they would get a C group or such, but I did not tell them what kind of group they were going to get until about two days before the end of the school year because I did not want any trouble with the teachers. When one teacher learned that she was going to get a C group she wept, said she hated it, but now she is perfectly contented and pleased and would probably do anything I want her to. This year I am going to make some changes and I do not intend to tell the teachers until the last moment. One day I saw another teacher in the hall before we had assigned groups and I started kidding her, asking her how she would like a C group, since she had had so much training in the manual arts, and she blew up and swore she would never take one. The children have no feeling against being in a C group, but the teachers feel—or did feel—that it degrades them.

Mr. Greer is proud of having instituted this system in Yankee City and wants it adopted in all schools. He says that the section system is based on the principle of "giving more individual attention." It seems, however, that the section system here functions so that the lower academic status of C section contributes to the lower social status of the lower-lower class.

The grammar-school principal acts as a sieve in selecting the students for the various high-school courses. In a predominantly lower-class school this is a difficult job, for it almost amounts to persuading the children to ignore the two highest status courses in the high school. In Table VIII we see the selection of high-school courses by the students themselves.

TABLE VIII

EIGHTH GRADE—DORLAND SCHOOL

(Student Selection of High-School Course)

Section	A	B	C
High School Curriculum			
Latin and Science	15	0	2
Commercial and General	11	31	25

The principal says:

The general course is just a course for kids who will dig ditches. The taxpayers will kick someday about continuing that course. [About the commercial course group, he says] The course is tough work, the A group kids will walk away with honors, however, and only the cream of the C group are in here.

About the two in the C group who elected the Latin course, he says "My job is to change this."

"For the Latin and scientific curricula," according to this principal, "a student must have great industry, but more important is that he be good in English, also in math, but he must be good in English. They have to take Latin, French, and German also in these curricula."

Mr. Greer does this job of "changing minds" about high-school courses by giving talks to the children in groups and by individual conferences. He described it thus:

At the present time I am endeavoring to do something with the graduating grades for their future life vocationally. You know the vocational-professional proportion is about 92 per cent to 8 per cent but our schools are training the whole 92 per cent as if they were to be members of the 8 per cent professional class. I am giving all the groups A, B, and C a talking to, explaining the disadvantages of the white-collar job to all of them.

It is surprising how many people in 8C want the prestige of a white-collar job. So I point out how poor the pay is and endeavor to point out how hard it is to fit oneself for such a job and to make a success of it; the majority of them are unfitted for any such work.

It is singular how many girls want to be teachers and nurses. It is strange that they do not, in this age at least, have any desire to become a stenographer; their great aim is to be a teacher or a nurse. Whenever I find girls who want to become nurses I describe to them just exactly what they would have to go through before they could become a regular nurse, telling them that they would have to scrub floors and that sort of thing at the beginning, and I go into all the gory details. I think this desire to be a nurse is due to the sort of romantic ideal of nursing which the girls of this age develop. Obviously the whole urge toward becoming a teacher is due to the system of education which they undergo, which, in itself, is adapted only to make more teachers. This educational system is a terrific waste of money and time to the city, since so few people can by any chance become members of the white-collar class and so many must follow some vocational line.

I've got to look after the eighth-graders because they will shortly graduate and be thrown on their own resources, either to go to high school or to work, and it is my business to see that they get some conception of what they are fitted for or what they can go into. I explain to them about the courses which are given in the high school, just what they are going into and what the courses and the systems of study really mean.

It is Mr. Greer's responsibility to prevent attempts at social mobility on the part of those who he thinks have poor chances and to persuade those who he thinks can "get ahead" to take the more difficult high-school courses.

The evidence from the Yankee City schools demonstrates that the school reinforces the class standards in the general community, from an early period in the child's life through high school and into college. Most lower-class children are placed in the lower academic sections and higher-class children tend to be put in the higher sections in elementary school. When they leave elementary school, most of the A section children elect high-school courses that are preparatory for college; few of the B and only a small number of the C section do. In high school the same tendency continues; the lower classes take commercial and general courses and the upper and upper-middle classes take college-preparatory work.

In Hometown the section system is not in use and in general there is less formal differentiation of students into separate ability groups or vocational groups than in Yankee City and Old City. Nevertheless, status considerations enter at certain points. For example, in an effort to "democratize" the school by doing away with the traditional marking system, Mr. Mercer, the principal, ran up against strong opposition. Instead of giving numerical marks Mercer instituted a system whereby children were to be graded as either unsatisfactory or satisfactory. He says, "When we tried that S and U system, it was the parents who are college graduates who opposed it. As a matter of fact, it wasn't satisfactory; I found teachers were using S as top, then S-minus, then U-plus and U and U-minus; you see what they did—they made a five-grade system out of it. I wanted to do away with grades entirely."

One of the more vociferous opponents of this innovation and most others is Judge Scott who has had two sons go through the high school and on to college. He said once, "I go down there and argue with 'em at times—I used to at least—now that the boys are older and in college I don't care so much. But I've gone down there and argued, and they just beam and beam and say, 'This is Life! This is Life!' Nuts! What they are doing in school isn't life. Why, one time they changed the marking system and decided to give S for satisfactory and U for unsatisfactory on the basis of 'effort.' They said 90, 80, 70 and so on was unfair because it didn't give credit for effort or progress . . ." When it was pointed out that he had a special interest in having his boys prepared for college, he replied, "Of course I want the school to prepare for college. When they tell me 'This is Life' I get sore. You don't get credit in life for *effort*—you get it for what you produce."

Judge Scott is expressing the dominant upper-middle and upper-class evaluation based on production. The experience of Judge Scott and his friends is that a person is judged on what he produces, not how hard he works. The men working on the "factory side" work hard but they do not produce the "right" things and so they do not "get ahead" which is the Law of Life in the upper-middle class.

In many school systems intelligence tests are used as a means of sectioning children according to ability. If an intelligence test measures "real" intelligence, we cannot say that discrimination on status grounds exists in these schools. But the intelligence tests generally used as a basis for grouping children are known to favor urban children with family backgrounds that encourage reading, travel, talking, museum visiting, and so on. The problems given and the vocabulary used in these tests are taken pretty largely from urban middle-class life. Accordingly, rural children and lower-class urban children do not do as well on these typical *verbal* intelligence tests as they do on *performance* tests of intelligence and on other tests in which efforts have been made to eliminate the factor of cultural background. And if pupils are grouped according to their showing on the usual verbal test of intelligence, the upper group will consist mainly of upper- and middle-class children.

Of course, there are exceptions to grouping on the basis of social class. The explanation of these exceptions falls in two parts. In the first place, there is no doubt that ability is frequently rewarded regardless of class. It is true though that the lower-class child must show greater ability to be recognized than does the higher-class child. Secondly, whenever a lower-class child shows in his behavior that he or she is quick to learn the middle-class standards of acting, the teacher is more likely to reward that child. Or if the child shows any exceptional talent, the teacher will act encouragingly. What appears to happen is that the teacher, like a speculator, puts her efforts and rewards where she thinks they will bring in the biggest gain. She knows that those who are most likely to succeed, here placed in their order of probability, are those from better-class families, those who have exceptional ability, and those who seem to have the stuff to learn the ways of living which make them comparable to children of the better-class families.

As previously pointed out, social mobility depends as much on "proper behavior" as on anything else. Children learn proper behavior as they learn other things by being rewarded for doing the correct thing or by being punished for doing the wrong thing. The teacher does a good deal of rewarding and punishing as she consciously or unconsciously encourages behavior according to middle-class standards.

Thus we see the school formally dividing its pupils into groups which have as part of their standards the social class position of the family and the class behavior of the child. Young people from families of a given social position learn to be with one another and to exclude those of lower social status.

How Children Teach Each Other Status Differences

Informally, the school is an arena where the class distinctions can be learned and made by the children themselves, using as criteria the things they learn at home and from the school. A specific example of this process of discrimination based on social status is found in the following episode described by a teacher in the elementary school in Old City:

I'll give you an instance of the way they feel. You know I have this little club in my grade and in June I took a group of them to the state capital. When I first asked them to sign up, I had twenty-one to go but when they finally got around to going there were only twelve, and all but one of those twelve were my A section socialites. The only little girl from B section almost didn't go and she took weeks making up her mind. She came and said she didn't think she could go and I urged her and asked her why not. She said, "Well, I just think I would feel funny going with those other girls. You know I don't go to the same places they do. They don't ask me to their parties and we are just different. I think I would feel funny about going with all of them." Well, I said to her: "Now, Marion, I don't think I would feel that way. We are all going to be together while we are there. I don't think you need to worry about it. I know all those girls are too well bred to be rude to you even if you don't go to the same parties they do. And you must remember that you are just as smart as they are and you dress just as nicely and you look just as nice all the time. I don't think you need to feel uncomfortable about it at all." She said: "Yes, ma'am, I know, but they just don't feel that way about it."

It is apparent throughout all kinds of groupings of children in school that this class factor plays an important part. In the clubs, if all the officers are from one group the others are loath to participate. Upper- and upper-middle class girls would not play on the basketball team in Old City because most of the players were from the lower-middle and lower classes. And so those children gradually learn to like their "own kind" and frown on the others. In other words, the children learn to "know their places" in the community.

The behavior learned in school is described well in the incident related by a home economics teacher in Old City:

> I usually let them give a little luncheon every now and then. They really do quite well at it, too. We have one of them as hostess and one as host. We usually have a teacher as a guest because that keeps them on their best behavior and then she will usually help keep the conversation running along smoothly, too. Of course we have to break one of the first rules of etiquette and let the hostess get up from the table because we don't have a tea wagon or anything resembling one. But I just have to explain that to them. I think it is awfully good training for them because most of them will probably do their own work when they have a home of their own and it is just as well for them to know.

This same teacher says she is

> supposed to teach them anything and everything. I try to give them a little about clothes and what is appropriate. I try to tell them what colors are good together and what sort of thing is appropriate for school wear and all that. . . . I try to show them what is right even if they can't always do it. I really do feel sorry for them because of course they don't all have the money to do it with. Then I try to teach them all kinds of etiquette, too.

In Yankee City there is not so much effort made in the elementary school to try to teach the lower-class children proper middle-class behavior, because the class lines are more rigid. The principal of the Dorland School is always making allowances in behavior, expecting less refined behavior from lower-class children. He does it by using a parent's standard of judgment. He punishes a child if he can expect an affirmative answer to the question: "Your father would be pretty mad if he knew what you have been up to?"

Distinctions in social status are less finely drawn among adolescents than among adults, thus allowing friendships to form more easily across class lines. School children of upper-middle class social positions have an opportunity to participate intimately with those of higher social status. Some middle-class individuals do not continue to participate with upper-class individuals in adult life; others, as they become adults continue this participation and at the same time pattern their behavior after that of the upper class. Such persons tend to be those with personality traits which make readjustments relatively easy. They do not settle back into conventional patterns of middle-class behavior in which their parents trained them.

The school, besides purveying knowledge to the children, keeps or helps to keep the children in groups according to social class. Thus, children learn to like being with people of their own class or higher and to dislike being with people of lower classes especially if the social distance is great.

It is to be always kept in mind, however, that besides tending to bring children up to "know their place" the school also gives to those who want them, and can use them, the techniques for upward mobility. The most essential requirement for this mobility is the ability to participate with those higher without being noticeably different, that is, "knowing how to behave." There are some attributes which are of special value for upward mobility. We find, for instance, that the good athlete, the talented musician, the brilliant student, or the pleasant personality can more easily get ahead. In addition, the teachers and the others who run the school system, generally being middle-class, tend to present many of the proper techniques to those who would or could use them. They do this by teaching polite behavior, chaperoning trips to the big city, and setting an example at local social affairs.

Status factors are important in the classroom. They help mold the life career of the growing child. They load the dice for or against him in accordance with his family's position in the community. But they are not the only factors which operate, since lower-class children do climb.

One of the functions of the school is to encourage a moderate amount of social mobility from the lower strata. At the same time the school acts to preserve the existing status differences among the majority of children.

CLASS AND A CHILD'S REPUTATION

Children evaluate their classmates. They choose their friends. They decide who is good-looking, who plays games well, who is a good fighter, who is a leader, who is quiet, who is noisy, who is teacher's pet, and they make a host of other judgments about each other.

A child's reputation among other children stems from a variety of sources: from his actual behavior; from what other people, especially parents and teachers, say about the child, and the way they behave toward him; and also from what older people think and say about the child's family and their associates. The reputations of Tom Brown, Bob Jones, Kenneth Peabody, and Joe Sienkowitz were not only well-established by the time they were in the fifth grade—they had already taken on the generalized reputations of the social class groups to which they belonged.

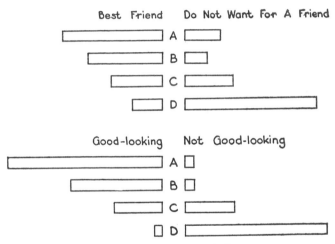

FIG. 1. SOCIAL CLASS AND A CHILD'S REPUTATION

Relative frequency of mention by social class, grades 5 and 6 (corrected for differences in size of social class groups)

How the family's social position enters into a child's reputation with his peers is a problem which we have investigated in Hometown.[1] Neugarten asked each child in the fifth and sixth grades to fill out a "guess-who" questionnaire, in which he wrote down the names of his age-mates who fitted certain thumbnail sketches, such as: "Here is someone who is a good fighter," "Here is someone who likes school very much." The responses to four statements are shown graphically in Figure 1. The four statements were:

These boys and girls are my best friends; they are the ones I play with most of the time.

These are the boys and girls I wouldn't want to play with.

Here is somebody who is thought to be very good-looking.

Here is somebody whom most people think is not good-looking at all.

The relative number of votes received by children of the various social classes are shown by the lengths of the bars. These numbers have been adjusted so as to equate the sizes of the social class groups. There were no children of the upper classes in these grades. Consequently groups A, B, C, and D correspond to upper-middle, lower-middle, upper-lower, and lower-lower, respectively.

It is clear from the graph that children of all social classes tend to want children of the higher levels for friends, and not to want children of the lower levels as friends.

Quite unexpected were the results on the "good-looking" items. Again, the children of the higher social classes were said to be good-looking, while those of lower social level were said to be not good-looking. Yet the fifth- and sixth-grade classrooms contained a number of blonde, blue-eyed Polish girls and stalwart, freckle-faced Scotch-Irish boys of lower-class families who would undoubtedly be picked as good-looking by adults who knew nothing of social backgrounds.

On the other items in the questionnaire the results were the same. Favorable descriptions elicited the names of higher-class children, while unfavorable descriptions elicited the names of lower-class children. Although the relationship may not have been explicit in their minds, these ten- and eleven-year-old children were obviously making judgments about each other on the basis of family social position. Many of these judgments would be grossly in error if tested by objective standards.

This generalization concerning reputation and social position has its exceptions, of course. A few—a very few—lower-class children received favorable mention by children higher in the social scale. Furthermore, a similar study made in the tenth and eleventh grades showed some outstanding cases of lower-class boys and girls who enjoyed favorable reputations.

The results of Neugarten's study are of particular importance since they demonstrate how class values and ideologies *unconsciously* operate in children, just as they *unconsciously* and consciously do in the lives of their parents. Few, if any, of the children studied realized they were making class judgments about their peers. Most of their parents are only infrequently aware of the ever-present class bias in their judgments of their neighbors, friends, and fellow citizens.

Since these children have acquired and organized sets of class attitudes at this early age, the question now arises, does child training by parents differ at the several social levels, and if so, what are the differences? Preliminary results of a statistical and interviewing study done by Evelyn Millis Duvall to answer these questions demonstrate that there are basic differences and that the nature of the differences lies in the effort by the parents to organize their children's lives to conform to the standards of the social level in which they live, or to prepare the children for social advancement.

Her study examines the parents' ideas of what constitutes a good and bad parent and a good and bad child. She secured data from parents at four social levels. This was done for Negroes and whites and among whites, for Jews and Gentiles. The results show that there are greater differences in the ideology of child training between the highest and lowest class levels for both races and for both creeds, than exist between the two races or the two creeds. In other words, upper-middle class Negroes, Jews and Gentiles are more alike in child-training ideology than are upper-middle and lower class whites, or upper-middle and lower class Negroes. The overwhelming majority of these parents were unaware that they were making class distinctions when they decided what made a good or bad parent. They believed they were concerned with moral, hygienic, and other standards that had nothing to do with status.

We can conclude from the studies of Duvall, Neugarten, and others cited in this book that class values are of the utmost importance in the training of children from the moment of birth throughout their growth and, in fact, throughout their lives.

CHAPTER VII

Social Mobility Through Education

MARTHA FROM BOXTOWN

So FAR we have seen how most growing children are fitted to their family's social position by the school in our society. But we have not examined how a few of them are elevated by the school from lower to higher strata. Yet a considerable number do rise. The brief life histories in the chapter on social mobility give us some knowledge of how people overcome these barriers to success. But none gives us a detailed picture of what happens when mobility through the school takes place. The case of Martha of Hometown will illustrate and bring out some of the chief points of successful mobility in the school and of a later rise in the community.

Martha's career is a story of upward social mobility by use of the school. It shows how Martha Totten, coming from a poor social background, was able by her own personal qualities and by the help of her mother and her teachers to rise to respectable middle-class position.

When Martha first appeared at school, she was a shy, thin, blonde child, looking like a fresh version of her pale, prematurely old, mother. Everyone knew she came from Boxtown on the wrong side of the tracks. Her father and Bob Jones' father were great cronies. Their drinking bouts were well-known and some of them were recorded on the police blotter. Martha's mother came to the school several times in the first few months to inquire about Martha's progress. This was enough to attract the attention of the teacher. But, in addition, Martha differed from the other Boxtown children in that her dresses, though faded and patched, were always clean. Martha was always serious. She seldom played noisy games and could usually be found in the classroom at recess, doing simple tasks for the teacher.

Since Martha and her mother were so exceptional for Boxtown residents, the teachers made some inquiries. They learned that

Martha was born on a small farm in northern Indiana. When Martha's father, Bob Totten, was killed in an accident, the folks in the community helped Mary Totten to run the farm, but the going was difficult and she had to give up the job of operating the farm. But then what? In this confusion it was not difficult for Jake Platt, the cheerful but irresponsible laborer who was employed on the farm, to convince Mary that she should marry him and move with him to Hometown. After Mary and Jake were married, Jake suggested sending Martha to relatives or an orphanage but Mary was adamant about keeping the child. It must have been with some misgiving that Mary moved her baby into the tar-paper shack in Boxtown.

In the first seven years of their marriage the Platts had five children. Mary hated this life but could find no escape. Her established rural background would not let her run from responsibility. Martha, the girl she brought to city filth from the farm, received most of her attention. She was going to do her best for the girl in spite of everything. She was going to do her best for the others, too, but after all Jake had to share some of the responsibility for them. Mary kept the shack as clean as she could. She sewed away at the ragged castoff clothing they received from the charity so that her children could go to school and be properly dressed. She ignored Jake, who spent any money he got on liquor and roistering.

Home for Martha was where she could be with her mother, and school was where she could be doing nice things with nice people. Martha's teachers could never quite understand her attachment to them because it wasn't of a sentimental, affectionate nature but rather a desire for their company and for doing the things they did or wanted to have done. As best she could, Martha became the teacher's pet although it might be more accurate to say that the teacher became Martha's pet. "Teacher's pet," she was called, and many another expression characterizing her obeisant attitude to school authorities and their standards was thrown at her. But Martha paid no attention to them. The favor of the teachers took the form of extra help of all kinds: in schoolwork, in leniency, and sometimes in gifts of books she could not afford to buy.

During the winter of her first year of high school Martha's mother died. Martha, frightened but resolute, took over her mother's responsibilities and tried to keep the children clean and respectable, while her stepfather wallowed deeper and deeper in the life of the river bottom. Jake Platt did not fear his stepdaughter as he had her mother. Martha had more and more trouble protecting the children from their father's drunken rages, especially since he had more freedom to use his relief check as he saw fit. Because of the visiting teacher's interest in Martha, the plight of the Platt family became known, and a woman's club adopted them for a time and gave them extra supplies of food and clothing. This allowed Jake to spend more of his relief money on liquor.

Martha did her best to counteract her stepfather, but she fought a losing battle with Boxtown. The children grew to be unrecognizable among the other Boxtown children. They disliked school, and in spite of the combined efforts of Martha and the visiting teacher they were often truant. All of them were "kept back" at one time or another, and when Martha encouraged them to work hard so that they could get into high school they shrugged their shoulders and let her know that high school had no attraction for them. In the shack where Mary Platt had slaved to keep things clean and respectable, the windows grew thick with rain-splashed dust, and the ragged curtains grew dirtier and dirtier. Windowpanes were broken and replaced by pieces of cardboard, junk collected in the yard, and the Platt home became outwardly the same as any other Boxtown hovel.

The visiting teacher and some of the high-school teachers arranged a scholarship for Martha to continue her education until graduation from high school. They saw to it that Martha got the necessary clothing and books and that her class dues and similar fees for school activities were paid. During her senior year in high school they became worried about her vocational future. In spite of some mild advice to the contrary, she had taken the academic course which would prepare her for college. Whenever her adviser suggested that it might be well for her to switch to the commercial course, she displayed a stubbornness that was almost unusual in her dealings with the teachers. There were a half dozen other Boxtown girls in the high school, and they were all taking the commercial course. Martha said to her adviser, "I'll find a way of earning my living. I need school for other things."

Martha developed one other interest. It was shortly after the school party in her sophomore year that she began attending the Young People's Society of the Methodist church, the Epworth

League. Every Sunday night after she had cooked an early supper for the children she dressed up and walked across town to the church, where she became known as a faithful but not active member of the Epworth League. When it was her turn, she took part in the program without attracting any particular attention. The other young people seemed to enjoy having her with them. They were all nice boys and girls, Martha thought. Some of them had dropped out of high school and were working while those who were still in school were the kind of people whom Martha felt drawn to. They were not active in the social life of the school, and they did not have money for expensive social affairs.

In her senior year Martha was persuaded to take a kind of apprentice course in merchandising, in which she spent two hours a day as a salesclerk in several stores. She took this course in the hope that it would help her get a job after graduation.

MARTHA CLIMBS OUT OF BOXTOWN

As graduation week passed and there was still no prospect of employment, the visiting teacher who had taken so much interest in Martha told her about Tom Brown's mother and father who were looking for a "nice girl who can stay with us and help out with the children." Tom was about six years old at the time, and Ellen was a baby. The Browns needed someone to stay with the children when they went out at night and to help a little bit with the housework. The job would pay only three dollars a week plus room and board, but it would give Martha an opportunity to live with nice people while she continued her attempts to find permanent employment in a store.

To Martha this was an opportunity—to live with respectable people in a house that would not smell of stale coffee and kerosene. But then she wondered what would become of her half sisters and half brothers. She felt responsible for them, even though she knew she had not been successful with them. She knew that things would grow much worse if her responsibility were turned over to Jake. For a moment she hesitated. Then her mouth tightened and her cold gray eyes hardened. "I'll take it," she said. "At least I can live like other decent people."

In the next few months Martha learned "the refined ways" of young business people. From the Browns she learned some of the niceties of living-room conduct. But she also learned some things which puzzled her. The magazines which the Browns had on the living-room table were strange to her, and she began to wonder whether the *Redbook* and *Cosmopolitan* were the best, as she had always supposed. She heard the Browns talk about going to see stage plays in Chicago as though they were superior to the movies in Hometown. And it seemed to Martha that the Browns didn't enjoy their home as much as they might. They spent so much time away from home. One night a week they played bridge at the house of friends. Usually twice a week they went out in their car and ate at a restaurant. Mr. Brown had a meeting of some sort at least one other evening. Mrs. Brown went out to the Women's Club every Tuesday afternoon. This was all strange to Martha, who thought to herself that if she ever had a home like this she would get more pleasure out of it.

She made every effort to get a permanent job at the Fair Store where she was employed as an "extra" but she did not succeed. She saw other girls taken on while she was kept on the "extra" list. She finally went to the manager and bluntly asked him why she had never been considered for permanent placement. The official studied her record card for some time and recognizing her determination he said, "If you really want to know, I'll tell you. In store work we look for people who can show enthusiasm for their work and instil customers with confidence in our store. Now every supervisor you have worked for as a student or as an extra has rated you as 'cold and impersonal.' I am sorry but we can on that basis hardly give you permanent employment."

Cold and impersonal—but in her life she had to be cold and impersonal. If she was going to survive, she had to be deliberate and even calculating. How could she have kept going ahead at all since her mother died unless she coolly chose her way—the right way, the hard way—instead of the easy, sentimental way?

The next significant episode is one about which our knowledge is only slender. Martha became acquainted with a magazine salesman who called at the door to sell magazines. He was nice to her and she liked him. Don Parker, the magazine salesman, took her to her first night club. She had a sweet liqueur, her first taste of an alcoholic drink, and learned that all "drinking was not horrible the way Jake did it." After several dates with him she learned that all kissing was not "necking" the way the Boxtown girls used to talk about it when they bragged of their conquests. She stayed out late at night with Don, and some of their time was spent in parking. Despite their growing intimacy, Martha was not physically thrilled by her relations with Don. She liked him because he dressed well, because he spoke good English, and because he had a good job. When she ultimately stayed all night with him, she did it because he wanted to marry her and marriage with him meant security and a nice home, and knowing people she respected.

Don Parker's business kept him in town for several months. Shortly after he left Hometown for his next station, Martha realized that she was going to have a baby. She immediately tried to get in touch with him. He had told her that he loved her and that he would come back to her. She sent him a registered letter which was forwarded to his next address and returned marked "not known at this address." The prospect of having an illegitimate child was nearly too much for Martha. After all her striving for respectability, here she was as bad or worse than her Boxtown fellows. How they would gloat over this!

She determined that she must handle this without anyone's finding out. In a few months she told Mrs. Brown that she was going back to Indiana to visit her mother's people. She went to a near-by city and entered a maternity home. Things were better there. The baby, a girl, was born in the summer, some four months after Martha entered the home. She was a beautiful child, and Martha soon became a devoted and proud mother and was determined to keep the baby. She dreamed of the life she would make for her daughter. More realistically she had to worry about what she was going to do with a baby. Other girls in the nursing home worried about the same thing. One girl suggested to Martha that she file a paternity case against Mr. Brown, her former employer. Martha replied, "But Mr. Brown is not the baby's father; besides, think of the reputation you get for yourself and the baby. Why, we'd be labeled for life." The other girls just could not understand this kind of behavior. Martha understood them—they were like the Boxtown gang. But all of Martha's respectability could not tell her what to do when her six months were up and she had to leave.

The superintendent of the nursing home, having found out quite a bit about Martha, got in touch with the Browns to see whether they could help. Mrs. Brown arranged for Martha to work in a household exchange store in Hometown, run by the social agency, where old furniture and clothing were sold. This job paid eight dollars a week. A room was found for Martha at two dollars a week. This left six dollars for food, clothing, and incidentals. Recreation was an impossibility. It was often necessary to choose between eating dinner and buying necessary stockings. In the meantime the baby was left in the nursing home.

Everybody expected Martha to give the baby up for adoption. But they had all guessed wrong. She explained to the Browns and to the superintendent of the home that the child was one of her responsibilities. When the superintendent told her that she would have to do something about the baby, she begged him to care for it until she could find another solution for the problem. This the superintendent agreed to do saying that the baby would have to be turned over to the juvenile court if no other plans were made within the year.

In the next few months Martha's salary was increased to twelve dollars a week. This enabled her to buy a few things for the baby, to visit her once a month, and to dress better. She began attending some affairs for business girls sponsored by a women's organization in Hometown. Here she learned to dance, and it was at a Dance Night program that she met Dick Johnson. Dick was a regular attendant at these affairs. He was the son of a local lawyer —not a prominent or a well-recognized attorney, just a run-of-the-mill courthouse lawyer. Dick was no intellectual giant. He had received low grades in high school and finally dropped out and learned radio repairing. Nor was he a handsome charmer. The oil and dirt of the radio sets he repaired always lingered on his hands, and he paid no attention to his clothes. Dick's intentions were obvious. He went to the dances "to get acquainted with some nice girls." Martha heard one of the girls say to another, "He thinks you want to marry him if you give him two dances." Martha danced with him most of the evening. She liked him. He had a respectable lower-middle class family, a steady job, and he liked to please her.

Martha understood that Dick could easily be prompted into a proposal and she deliberately led him on. She had several dates with him. She knew that her course was cold and deliberate, but she also knew that she would make a good wife for Dick. The night he proposed she told him about the baby. She was surprised and happy at his willingness to take the baby too. In fact, Dick suggested that he legally adopt the child. This was all Martha could ask.

In the short time they were engaged, they found a white house with a garden—a house quite like the one that Martha had often dreamed about. It was far from Boxtown, and as Dick put it, "It's in a good neighborhood."

They were married in June. The ceremony was conducted by the Methodist pastor. It was a quiet affair at the home of Dick's parents, who were the only ones there. They drove in Dick's car to their new house, and Dick was pleased and proud when Martha burst into tears as they entered their new home.

Martha had climbed from her Boxtown beginnings and stabilized her life in the middle class of Hometown. What can be learned from Martha's career?

Martha was born to a father and mother who were small farmers of upper-lower class status. They had the solid virtues, respectable behavior, and ambitions of the small farmer. When Martha's father died and her mother remarried, Martha and her mother dropped to the level of Boxtown. Martha's mother did not succumb to the life around her. Part of Martha's ambition was the result of her mother's teaching her precepts and principles of life from their former social level.

Martha's mother set a pattern and a goal for her, but had Martha not found help in school, she could never have held out. Martha was an exception among lower-class children. Most lower-class children do not understand or appreciate the teacher's efforts. In turn, the teacher tends to neglect the lower-class children if she does not actually discriminate against them. They do not reward her with obedience and affection, and she does not reward them with affection, good marks, and special approval. Conversely, when the teacher finds a lower-class child who does respond to her efforts, who does seem to understand middle-class standards, she is the more interested and puts in extra effort where she thinks she can do some good. Certainly this is what happened to Martha. Not only, then, was Martha ready to make the most of school, but the school was ready to do its best for her. She exemplifies an American ideal—to get ahead no matter what the obstacle— "never say die"—"anyone can get ahead if they only try." And Martha had many hardships, some of them almost impossibly high: where she lived, her playmates, her stepfather, economic deprivation, her mother's death, Marybelle, her younger half sisters and half brothers, misdirection in her education so that she had no vocation, an illegitimate child.

For Martha the school was indispensable for achieving her purpose. It taught her the things she would have to know, it showed her the details of refinement, and through the school the world of respectability opened up.

Throughout this story we get suggestions of Martha's outstanding characteristic—coldness. This was both her strength and her weakness. It was her strength because it enabled her to hold out against the sentimental, easygoing life of Boxtown and against the disapproval of many of her lower-class age-mates. Eventually it enabled her to free herself from her half brothers and half sisters in spite of her strong sense of responsibility. Martha had to calculate the consequence of every act if she were to get ahead. Even the affair with the magazine salesman may have been entered into coldly. We do not know enough about it to say definitely. There are suggestions all through her career that sexually Martha was not responsive.

But coldness and reserve were also a handicap, as Martha learned when she attempted to get a job in the department store. The Brown family, though they could find nothing wrong with the way she did the housework, were relieved to have her go. In her own home it will be interesting to observe Martha. Will she become a warmhearted, affectionate wife and mother? Or will she continue to drive herself and her husband and her child ahead, living always in the future?

If we allow ourselves to speculate a bit about Martha and Flora Belle, we can see that Martha resembles Flora Belle's mother— "an orphan" partly reared by another family. Mrs. Bennett was extremely aggressive. She married a man whom she hoped to make over into something she wanted and who had all the fundamentals of respectability. Mrs. Bennett moved from lower class to middle class. Her daughter, Flora Belle, moved from middle class to upper class.

Because of Martha's appreciation of her teachers and all they stood for, we might even speculate that Martha's daughter might be influenced into becoming a teacher and follow a path similar to that of Flora Belle.

Martha went ahead with ruthlessness and an indomitable drive —rarely looking back and always looking ahead. She did not figure things out, but she knew that she wanted the nice things of this world. Her choices were always between getting ahead or going all the way back to Boxtown. The thought of Boxtown was a whip urging her forward.

Flora Belle was always careful. She went a step at a time, never giving up anything she had gained until she was secure above. But Flora Belle carried no such load as Martha did.

Education for Martha and Flora Belle was the path to success. For Martha, however, education was really learning things she wanted to know and could use. For Flora Belle, education was an arena for her ambitious activities. Education, as we have already pointed out, is oriented to the middle class and therefore attracts mobile lower-class people. At the same time, it tends to push ahead the mobile middle-class person; therefore education has different meanings and works on different principles for people of different classes.

CHAPTER VIII

Teachers in the Status System

Miss Virginia Crane sat at her desk and read the letter for the third time. There, in black and white, was the proof that she had achieved her life's ambition. "I wish to offer you the position of Critic Teacher in our Laboratory School at a salary of $1,800." The letter was signed by the president of the State Teachers' College. This meant that, at twenty-eight, she had made such a success of teaching that she was recognized as a master teacher, fit to show others how to teach.

She looked around the schoolroom, which was pleasant, warm, and homey in the slanting rays of the late afternoon sun. After all, the schoolroom was a home to her, and the children were her children. She looked across the empty desks. Each one seemed to retain some of the personality of its occupant. Katherine Green's desk, on one side of the room, was neat and orderly, and seemed rather distant from its neighbors. Tom Brown's desk, second from the front, had a piece of paper sticking out where Tom had left it in his rush to go out and get started in a game. Bob Jones' desk, in the back row, had a big ink spot on it. She knew that if she looked inside she would find little equipment for learning—only a couple of dirty books and a grimy pad of paper.

So this would be her last year in Hometown. Next fall she would move to the college town where she had once been a student, and she would settle down there in a pleasant little house, bringing her parents to live with her. She thought back comfortably over her life, relishing each picture that came to her mind.

She remembered the one-room school where she had gone until she was thirteen. She did well in school, and during the last couple of years she helped the teacher with the little children. When she finished the grades, she went to stay with an aunt and uncle in town while she attended high school. She thought of the good times at church socials and class parties. She thought of her special friendship with a boy whose father kept a store in town. Summers she helped her mother on the farm, always with a thought about school again in the fall. During the winter of her last year in high school, her English teacher asked her what she was going to do when she was graduated. Virginia was seventeen then. Her father advised her to take a business-college course and get a job as stenographer or bookkeeper in a local business. Her mother wanted her to become a teacher. Her English teacher advised her to go to normal school—only a few miles away—since her family could not afford to send her to college.

Virginia and a classmate, Helen Bond, went to normal school together and shared a room. Most of their food came from home, to which they returned at least once a month. At the end of the year both girls got positions in rural schools. Virginia taught for two years in the little white wooden schoolhouse not far from her home, and then she decided to change and look for a better position. She found that more training was required before she could hope for a much better job. Thus she started a series of summers at the State Teachers' College. After two more years she secured a position in an elementary school in a town of 2,500 population. This paid enough to enable her to take a full year off and graduate with a college degree at the age of twenty-six. Then she was offered a position in Hometown, where for two years she taught the fifth grade. She liked the children, and she was sure that people thought well of her. She would be sorry to leave Hometown.

Virginia felt both strange and familiar in Hometown. She joined the Baptist church and taught a Sunday-school class and sang in the choir. The minister often said that they could not get along without "the talents of Miss Crane." She belonged to the Women's Club and was something of a leader in its literary activities. But somehow she never got to know anyone—except teachers. She was beginning to think that she would always be a stranger wherever she lived.

It was even strange at home, during the brief summer weeks between the close of summer school and the opening of her own school in September. She liked to help her mother get the meals for the men during the threshing season, and she loved to put on a sunbonnet and work in the garden, but she had no real friends outside of her family. The girls and boys with whom she had grown up were either married and busy with their children, or, like her, they had gone out into the world and become insubstantial subjects of Sunday afternoon conversation for the older people. The boy whom she had liked so well in high school was running his father's store and had a wife and two youngsters.

Last summer Virginia had gone to the State University and started to work for an M.A. degree. At a church party for graduate students she had met a man who was working toward a Ph.D. in zoology. They had several dates and found that they liked each other very much. On the last few dates he had kissed her. She still felt queer all through her body at the thought of those kisses. They had written to each other. He was wrapped up in his work—that was clear from his letters. Well—she had her work and her career to think about, too. She hoped that he would be back at the university next summer. But she would have enough to think about whether he was there or not.

Next year she would find a nice house in the college town for her parents. Her father was going to give up the farm to her older brother. She would help make life comfortable for her father and mother. It would be pleasant, too, having a house to live in instead of a bedroom in someone's else house.

Virginia would be sorry to leave Hometown. Through observing and teaching the children she had come to know and like the place and its people. She had said to her sociology teacher once that she could tell what a community and its people were like from studying its children. For example, she had never met Mr. and Mrs. Peabody, but from observing Kenneth she knew that the Peabodys would be distant people. She had no desire to become better acquainted with them. She knew Mrs. Brown quite well, for they both worked in the Baptist Sunday school. She felt that she was fairly close to the Browns, though she had never been in their home. From trying to teach Bob Jones, and from comments of the other teachers about his older brothers, she had a pretty good idea of what the Jones family was like. "There are many like them in every town," she thought, "and school is the best influence in their lives. But mostly the school fails to improve them very much."

With these reflections Virginia Crane enjoyed herself as she fingered the letter which told her that she was a success in life. She had started from a social position of approximately upper-lower[1] status and had achieved a secure lower-middle status. She might go on to upper-middle if she cared to and worked hard enough at it. She was typical of thousands of successful teachers whose social participation we shall now describe briefly.

THE SOCIAL PARTICIPATION OF TEACHERS

The rather limited data at present available indicate that teachers are in the middle class and that many of them have risen from lower status. In the East and the South, where class lines have been established longer, the teachers are usually in the upper-middle class, and many of them have risen from lower-middle class families. In the Middle West and the West, the teachers are usually lower-middle class, and many of them have risen from lower-class families. Table IX shows the distribution of the public-school teachers among the social classes in Yankee City, Hometown, and Old City (white teachers only).

TABLE IX

SOCIAL CLASS DISTRIBUTION OF TEACHERS

	Hometown Per Cent	Yankee City Per Cent	Old City Per Cent
Upper upper	0	2	2.5
Lower upper	0	1	2.5
Upper middle	26	76	72.5
Lower middle	72	21	20.0
Upper lower	2	0	2.5
Lower lower	0	0	0.0
	100	100	100.0

Indirect evidence concerning the social position of public-school teachers can be obtained from studies of the social background of students in teachers' colleges. Tables X and XI report the occupations of parents and the religious affiliations of women students in fifteen widely distributed teachers' colleges, in the year 1929.

The parents of teachers, according to Table X, are largely farmers and businessmen. It is safe to say that the businessmen are mostly owners of small businesses—grocers, druggists, and the like. Quite a few teachers also come from the homes of skilled workers.

Two Protestant denominations, the Methodist and Baptist,

TABLE X

OCCUPATIONS OF PARENTS OF 1,080 WOMEN STUDENTS IN FIFTEEN TEACHERS COLLEGES[2]

Type of Occupation	Per Cent Engaged in Occupation
Professional	8.4
Manufacturing	3.1
Business (proprietary)	42.1
Farming	45.2
Public Service	4.5
Business (clerical)	5.0
Skilled Labor	14.8
Unskilled Labor	4.0

account for one-half of the prospective teachers reporting religious affiliation in Table XI. These two churches, more than any other Protestant denominations in the country, are middle-class.

TABLE XI

RELIGIOUS AFFILIATION OF 1,080 WOMEN STUDENTS IN FIFTEEN TEACHERS' COLLEGES[3]

Denomination	Per Cent
Methodist	25.7
Baptist	17.0
Presbyterian	8.6
Church of Christ (Disciples)	7.3
Roman Catholic	5.5
Lutheran	4.4
Episcopal	2.6
Jewish	2.5
Congregational	2.3
Friends	1.0
No affiliation	1.2
Did not answer question	27.0

In his study of the American schoolteaching profession, Elsbree shows that for the past hundred years schoolteachers have come mainly from a single socio-economic group which he calls "lower middle." He makes the following statement about teachers as a group:

The environmental limitations surrounding prospective teachers are the most serious handicaps confronting the profession. Coming as they do mostly from the lower-middle class, they bear all the marks of this relatively unfavored social and economic group. To fill in these cultural gaps in the experiences of teachers is a task of considerable magnitude. If it is to be done, the teacher-training institutions will have to assume the major responsibility. The hope of attracting into teaching any sizable group of individuals from the higher economic classes in American society seems futile. The task before the profession is the selection of individuals, regardless of the particular layer of social and economic strata from which they happen to spring, who possess the intellectual and personal potentialities essential for teaching success, then to surround them with an environment which reeks with cultural opportunities and experiences. Through such a process of osmosis, American teachers may achieve a professional and cultural level beyond the dreams of present-day educators.[4]

The social position of teachers is indefinite. Their social participation is often limited to their own professional group. The Hometown high-school principal said of his teachers, "They don't fit in much anywhere—they stay pretty much to themselves." The unmarried Hometown female teachers live together in groups of two to five, either boarding or renting apartments. Where social participation is used as the test of social status, the teachers are difficult to locate in the social structure because they participate so little in the social life of the community.

A man's participation is more nearly normal for his class position than is a woman teacher's. For example, Joe Grant, the teacher of commercial subjects in Hometown high school, is prominent in the Elks, where he enters into all the convivial activities including poker playing and beer drinking. A prominent man, commenting on this, said, "Well, it is this way. The Elks needed a man in there who could raise money for anything and Joe can do it." Regarding this same teacher, Mr. Mercer, the school principal, said, "Joe Grant seems to get around town more than other teachers; even more than other men teachers. Even though he drinks beer and takes a highball occasionally he is discreet." Joe is able to participate in many of the leading organizations and might be called an "organization man." In this way he is able to consolidate himself in the community and become more of a real member of the community than the other teachers.

In Hometown only one woman teacher, who was engaged to a local lawyer, was ever invited to parties given by members of the younger set. She took part in all the activities, including dancing, smoking, and drinking cocktails. But everyone knew that she would not be a teacher after the wedding and excused her.

Attitudes toward the high-school principal exemplify the

dominant attitude of Hometown toward educators. Mrs. Scott, an upper-class lady and wife of Judge Scott, both of whom are powerful as social arbiters in Hometown, says:

> Don't you like Mr. Mercer? Isn't he a grand person? You should have seen him when he came here—a tall, rawboned country boy. You know he came here as assistant coach and mounted right up. He wanted to be a brother to the boys and mixed with them—told them to call him Andy. I asked him what he was going to do about it when he was made principal. "You can't have all the boys calling you Andy," I said. And he said, "You know, I've thought about that, but there is nothing I can do about it now."
> Mrs. Mercer has come out a lot since she came here. They were both kids when they came to Hometown—met in normal school—country, you know, and she never raised her head to say anything. She's shy.
> I remember when Andy first tried to talk at meetings; he couldn't handle himself at all. Would sit on the edge of the table and swing his foot. And the most awful striped shirts! Striped, you know. Now he can make a nice talk and has developed some poise. Everybody likes him—they always have.

There is a feeling among people of the middle-class position and higher that a teacher is a strait-laced person and is likely to put constraint upon a party or other informal gathering. We hear in Old City such statements as, "Of course, his sister is out there a lot of the time now and she is a terrible stick. She is a schoolteacher, and doesn't drink, and they can't have much fun when she is around." With exceptions in the cases of a small proportion of men, a teacher's participation at a given class level always seems to be restricted to the ultrarespectable side.

The moral standards of the teaching profession are largely enforced from within. One afternoon at a tea an interviewer doing research in Old City told a teacher, "You all don't know what you are missing not smoking with your tea." And the teacher replied:

> Well, it is really my profession that keeps me from it. I haven't taught school anywhere that I wasn't asked not to smoke. When I came here the superintendent didn't really ask me not to smoke, though, of course, he asks us not to smoke in front of our students or at the school. But he was a very good friend of my brother-in-law's, and so when I came he said to me, "I know you have come from a schoolteaching family, so I guess there are a lot of things I won't have to tell you about your behavior that I would have to tell most new teachers." So I guess I missed a lot of his moral lectures.

The school superintendent must take responsibility for the social behavior of the schoolteachers. The superintendent of Old City is an upper-middle class man who has been mobile upward. He is a "good citizen" and one year received the Service Club trophy as "the most useful citizen." He does not approve of many of the social activities of the upper-uppers, lower-uppers, and some of his own class, especially the parties at which there is a good deal of drinking and other "sophisticated" activity. When a teacher was asked whether the school superintendent was strict or strait-laced, she said, "Well, yes, I think he is, though I don't think he is any more so than most superintendents. He doesn't approve of smoking and dancing, I know, though he doesn't condemn them. He just reflects the general attitude throughout the teaching profession."

PERSONALITY DIFFERENCES AMONG TEACHERS

Lest we get too narrow a picture of the teacher, let us look at the career of Miss Crane's former classmate and roommate, Helen Bond. Helen was a good student, though never quite so good a student as Virginia Crane. But Helen was more of a leader in student activities. Helen's father was the coal and feed merchant in the town where she and Virginia went to high school. He wanted to give Helen every advantage and was disappointed when his business slumped and he was not able to send her to college as she wished. Still, he could afford to keep her at home for a year or two "until she sets up a home of her own." He was surprised and somewhat disappointed when she announced that she was going to teach school. But she had always wanted to do things her own way, and he admired her spirit.

Thus it was that Helen went off with Virginia to normal school. At the end of the year she got a school out in the country. She lived with an elderly farm couple near by. She entered into the home, helping about the house and taking part in the entertaining of visitors. Soon she was invited to all kinds of social affairs, such as church suppers and barn dances. She was a leader in social activities, popular alike with the young men and the girls of the community.

Helen enjoyed her year of teaching but she still wanted to go to college. With an uncle's assistance she enrolled the next year at the State Teacher's College. Here she had a busy and happy time. She was elected to the highest student offices that a girl could hold. At graduation she found a position in a small suburb of a large city, teaching eighth grade. She boarded in the home of the parents of one of her fellow teachers, and in this way she was introduced quickly into the social life of community. In the city she attended concerts, theaters, and lectures, and she did her shopping in the big department stores. She joined the Episcopal church and took part in social activities connected with the church. The parents of her pupils liked her, and often invited her to their homes for dinner.

After two years of suburban life, Helen began to think about changing. She registered with a teachers' agency and soon was offered a job in Denver, teaching in a new junior high school. This sounded interesting, and she accepted the offer. She took with her some names of friends of her suburban acquaintances and when she arrived she found invitations awaiting her. News of her social interests and abilities had preceded her, and the Episcopal church found all sorts of things for her to do.

At one of the church functions she met George Turner, one of the leading young lawyers in town. He was older than Helen, distinguished in manner, bearing, and dress. In February they were engaged, with announcements and pictures in the newspapers. In June they were married. Helen's father and mother came to Denver for the wedding, which was held in the Episcopal church. If Mr. Bond was overawed by the Gothic arches and windows of the stately church, he did not show it. He carried his part of the ceremony with dignity. There was the same light of pride in his eyes and in the eyes of George Turner as they looked on the young woman who had brought them together. They gave each other a man-to-man handshake when the wedding was over. Mr. Bond said to his wife when they returned to their hotel room, "Well, I always did like her spirit. Even if I couldn't help her much, she always got what she wanted." At twenty-six, Helen had achieved her life's ambition, though she had never thought of it that way.

Helen Bond Turner joined the Women's Club and became chairman of the Entertainment Committee in a few months. Her name was frequently mentioned on the women's page of the newspaper. She aided her husband greatly in the political career upon which he had started. The Turners moved up quickly in the relatively mobile society of Denver. Helen Bond started from a position at the lower-middle level of a society like that of Denver (though her family was relatively higher in their small home town) and, through her own talent and personality, combined with her marriage, soon achieved an upper-middle status with a prospect of moving still higher.

When we compare the life stories of three teachers—Virginia Crane, Helen Bond, and Flora Belle Bennett—we see that social mobility meant different things to them, and they used different methods of rising to higher status. Virginia moved from lowly jobs to better jobs with higher rank in the teaching profession. Upward progress within the profession was her goal. This kind of progress led to a higher social position in the community, but Virginia did not care particularly for that. She will be content to participate at a kind of indeterminate middle-class level in the college town where she will teach.

Helen Bond and Flora Belle Bennett used teaching as a means of achieving higher status in the community. Though different in personality, these two young women used the same social mechanism to advance themselves. They had no ambition to become outstanding teachers, but the teaching profession gave them social contacts with the "best people," where their social talents could operate in their favor.

We do not attempt to explain why these three women took their different ways in life. For clues to the differences in the strivings and the satisfactions of these three human beings, we should have to delve more deeply into the social and biological factors which made them different persons.

THE SOCIAL ROLE OF THE TEACHER

On the immense stage of the North American continent boys and girls are born, grow up, and play their parts as adults. Helping them to learn their parts in the drama of life are the teachers, who themselves have a special role to play.

Teachers represent middle-class attitudes and enforce middle-class values and manners. In playing this role, teachers do two things. They train or seek to train children in middle-class manners and skills. And they select those children from the middle and lower classes who appear to be the best candidates for promotion in the social hierarchy.

Two groups of children escape this influence in part. Children of upper-class parents often do not go to the public schools or drop out after a few years of public-school attendance. These children attend private schools or have private tutors. The tutors and teachers in private schools are also usually middle-class people, but their role is not the same as that of the public-school teachers. They are restricted to teaching certain skills which have upper-class value. They are not expected to teach manners and social attitudes. Many children of lower-class parents also escape the influence of teachers, through being recalcitrant in school and through dropping out of school just as early as possible. But the teachers play their special role in the lives of the vast majority of American children, including all middle-class children and a great many lower-class children.

To play the teacher's role successfully and with a feeling of personal satisfaction requires a certain kind of personality. We have seen some of the characteristics of this personality. Many, probably most, teachers are using their profession to "get ahead in the world." They have either been born into the middle class or they have worked up into this class. Middle-class standards of refinement and ambition mean a great deal to them. They take these things seriously. They inevitably, and for the most part unconsciously, judge their pupils by these standards.

The teaching group perpetuates itself. Teachers are chosen, or choose their profession, largely through a kind of informal apprenticeship. Young people do well in school, they like their teachers, and they are liked by their teachers and encouraged to go into the profession. In turn, when they become teachers, they choose others like themselves to follow in their footsteps.

There are other possible social roles for a teacher, and we find a minority of teachers adopting them. There is the role of social reformer, played by a few teachers, usually men. This is a middle-class role, but it involves the teacher in conflicts with various middle-class interests in the community and sometimes ends in open hostility on the part of the school board and many parents toward the teacher. But if he is tactful and can stand the strain of the conflict, the teacher may succeed in playing this role, especially if he is a high-school teacher. Some teachers who play this role get opportunities to go into college teaching, where they are much more free to follow their particular variation of middle-class behavior.

The teachers in a large city school system have still another variation of the basic middle-class role. Where they are protected by tenure legislation, they have freedom to become active workers for certain underprivileged groups. They often join the teachers' union and work politically with groups which draw largely from the upper-lower level. This might lead teachers to abandon a middle-class role and to throw in their lot with a "class-conscious" lower class, bringing them in direct conflict with middle-class groups. But it has not happened. The American Federation of Teachers has been conservative of middle-class values, and teachers with thoroughgoing middle-class attitudes feel at home in the union.

It is difficult to conceive the teachers' social role in America as being anything but an expression of middle-class values. Unless there is a social revolution which upsets the middle class, teachers will continue to act as exemplars for this social class. But the middle-class viewpoint will change a great deal during the social changes of the next few decades. The naïve ideal of unlimited material progress for the society and unending social climbing for all its members who are industrious and ambitious is bound to give way to a more realistic view of society and of human nature, combined with greater faith in spiritual as opposed to material values. The role of the teacher as the exemplar for this philosophy will become more subtle and more creative.

CHAPTER IX

The Administrative Hierarchy

SUPERINTENDENTS AND PRINCIPALS

WE HAVE presented material showing how teachers and students interact in the social status system in America. We have seen, too, how social mobility affects the lives of teachers and students in school.

The administrative hierarchy of the school also is related to the social class system in ways important for education. What are some of the problems created in and for the school system by the fact that school administrators live in and are affected by the status system? In Chapter V we have seen a glimpse of how a principal, Mr. Mercer, functions in the status system of Hometown. From Yankee City we have more fully drawn portraits of two administrators in the school hierarchy and their relations to the status system.

The principal of the Dorland School is Mr. Greer. As the senior principal of the elementary school, he has a status within the school system next to that of the superintendent of schools.

Mr. Greer is about forty years old. He was born in a town near Boston where his father was a bookkeeper in a large factory, with a social status in the lower-middle class. The younger Greer did well in school. He was well-liked and studious. He was extremely short and undersized. This seems to be one reason for his great drive to succeed and get things done. When he was graduated from high school, he won prizes for his work in English and a scholarship to Brown University. But his father could not afford to give him any financial assistance, and Greer got a job as a reporter on a newspaper. After a year of this, his grandmother offered to help him in college. He went to Brown University for three years, but then his grandmother died and he could not continue in college. He returned to Boston and entered a secretarial school where he learned typing and shorthand. After six months

110

he was hired as a teacher in the secretarial school. While teaching in the school he took courses at the Normal School. Then the United States entered the war and Greer tried to join up, but he was rejected because of his small size. He finally got a job as a civilian in one of the war services.

After the war he took some courses at the universities around Boston such as Tufts and Northeastern. He made his living teaching secretarial subjects. Through special courses taken at Northeastern, the Y.M.C.A. College, Greer got into boys' club work. He married a girl he had met doing this work.

After a few years, Greer became ill and the doctors prescribed a complete change. So he bought a place in New Hampshire which he farmed for a few years. In a neighboring town there was a lot of trouble among the school board, the parents, and the teachers. Mr. Greer was hired as principal to clear it up because he was a member of the community in good standing, a successful farmer, and had had good business experience. He stayed there for three years. When a difficult situation arose in Yankee City, a mutual friend of Greer and a Yankee City school board member told the school board about Greer, how he had been in business, taught, and run a farm. So he was hired as principal of the Dorland School. In the three years he has been in Yankee City he has reached the maximum salary paid to principals —$2,400 a year.

We might call Mr. Greer a self-made man. Not only has he reached a fairly high position in the teaching profession but he has done so without going through the usual educational routines. This puts him in a peculiar conflict situation. He likes educational work because in it he has been a success, but he cannot go further in the profession (i.e., become superintendent of the school system) without meeting some of the academic requirements. We hear him say, "I've decided to quit. I'm looking around for a job where I can get ahead. I haven't had a chance in this system. I really hate to leave. I love this work, but I am dissatisfied at the same time." Another time he talks about finishing his academic training. "I wonder whether it would be worthwhile to get a degree. I've really come to the conclusion that I really do like teaching after all, and I expect I'll be a teacher all the rest of my life, so I guess I'll have to go through all the forms and take my degree."

Mr. Greer is an ambitious man who is sensitive about his background, his physical size, and lack of the correct symbols for advancement in teaching. However, he is a successful principal. His school is predominantly lower-class, and it is his job to fit these lower-class children into the middle-class school pattern. Mr. Greer says: "The principal is the connecting link between the school and the people of the community it serves. It is his job to adjust difficulties between parents and the school." More specifically, he describes his job thus:

The most common type of trouble with parents over a child is due to lack of ability to achieve in schoolwork. I like to handle all parent cases instead of letting the teachers do it. The average parent can best be approached by recalling his own school experience. He delights in it. Also you must attempt to get him to see the problem from the child's viewpoint. The average parent doesn't understand that a child lives in another world. Teachers also suffer from the same complex. In the many years of my experience parents have been called in only six times in disciplinary matters. I always try to meet the parents of a slow child, but there's no particular need to meet the parents of a bright child. The slow child is the problem. Often you cannot do anything with the parents. Many times parents have an inferiority complex. An inferior parent doesn't show interest in the child, whereas a bright parent usually will take a great deal of interest in the child. Difficulties often occur with the dull child of a bright parent. The parent dislikes to admit that the inferior child is related to him. It hurts his pride and he hates to admit that there's anything wrong with the child. The parent is perfectly able to understand the situation when it is someone else's child that is in difficulty. It helps a great deal to tell of disagreeable experiences which you have had with your own child. This makes the parent feel better and enables him often to grasp what you're driving at, helps his pride.

He sees his function as steering his students along the path best suited to them, and he steers them in a manner he considers most influential. If we could be present when he was advising them on their high-school careers—one of his more important jobs—we would witness a scene like this, as reported by the interviews:

A boy came in and was obviously quite frightened. Greer said, "Well, Frank, I had you in here a year ago for something, didn't I?" And Frank said, "I didn't do anything. I wasn't in here." Then Greer said, "Well, where did we talk?" The boy shrugged his shoulders. He was very scared. He wouldn't admit that Greer had ever seen him before for disciplinary purposes. Greer then said, "Well, what are you planning to do next year?" The boy said, "Don't know." "Going to high school?" "I don't think so." "Why?" "Too hard." The boy was sobbing and crying and wiping tears out of his eyes with his fist. And Greer said, "Here, stop your crying, you're not a baby, you're sixteen years old aren't you? What course are you going to take in high school?" He went on, "You're going to take a commercial course, aren't you? Well, you've done fair work in arithmetic, you have an

average of 67 and I'm going to give you a diploma. Feeling better now?"
The boy said, "Yes." "You watch your step. If you raise the deuce up there,
you'll sail in four months. But you've shown spurts of interest this year and
because you've chosen a commercial course, I'm letting you through. You're
entered on condition. You've got to watch your English and literature."

Mr. Greer is proud of the way he can as a school principal
steer his way through the difficulties of the New England social
system. Although he is not an adaptable man in the common sense
of that term, he is able to understand the standards and behaviors
of all social classes and act on the basis of that understanding.
He "sold" the section system to school authorities and to his
lower-class parent group with the same argument, "individual
attention," but with the school board he accented the "getting
ahead—not being pulled back" angle and with the parent group
he stressed "getting the most out of school," thus appealing to
slight but important differences of interest.

To do this with lower-class parents so that they and the school
board and those whom they represent are satisfied, Mr. Greer
must be someone who can take responsibilities without endanger-
ing his own social position. One way he does this is to have little
contact in the social life of Yankee City. He says, "I don't like to
get involved. I live far out in the country and I like to stay at
home with my wife and daughter or have a friend or two out to
visit."

Mr. Greer is successful in his capacity as an intermediator
among the social classes. He is a lower-middle class person, mobile
to upper-middle class, and what he wants most is security in the
upper-middle class and secure personal status. However, he does
not want to participate in the whole society of Yankee City. He
could not have the security he wants there because of his background and lack of definite professional training. Within the profession he finds the status denied him in the larger social sphere,
because he runs his lower-class school so successfully. Although
Greer can be a senior principal he cannot be superintendent of
schools because that requires advanced academic work. He realizes
this and considers working at summer school to get "the string of
letters after his name." In spite of the fact that he knows he cannot at present compete for the superintendent's office, Greer and
the superintendent are antagonistic to each other.

Bradford Keller is the superintendent. He is an upper-middle
class man moving into many lower-upper class groups. Mr. Kel-

ler's father was a civil service employee living in Maine. He had a responsible position as an accountant. Bradford was a mediocre student in school. He played football and basketball in high school. He went on to the University of Maine without thinking about it much. It was something his father had done and it seemed his teachers all counted on it. He took a general arts course at the university, specialized in mathematics, and played on the football team. He joined a good fraternity and became an officer in the R.O.T.C. At graduation he was advised by his counselor to take some work in education. His athletic experience would be valuable in the teaching profession, he was told. He acquired a Master of Arts degree in education and was given a position teaching in a high school in a small community in southern Maine. He taught mathematics in the ninth and tenth grades and was the athletic coach. He had a good football team. When an opening for an assistant coach developed in Yankee City, a member of the school board who had vacationed near the Maine community where Keller taught suggested him, and he was hired.

In the next three years the Yankee City high school team was turned into a winning team and credit was given to Keller for this achievement. However, no advancement could be given to Keller because of the tenure of the senior coach, and so Keller accepted a job with more money as an assistant coach in a large town. Keller attended education courses at Harvard during two summers. As football coach in Yankee City he had made many friends there. He was an important liaison man between school and community and when, after he left, the football team did not have much success the name of Keller, "the man who had the winning teams," frequently occurred in conversations. When a new superintendent of schools was to be appointed, Keller's name was put forward. He was known and liked by the members of the school board. He had all the qualifications and was a "good man for the community." "He had done advanced work in education" at Maine and at Harvard "everybody liked him," and he was appointed.

Keller is a tall, light-haired man with a rather flushed face. He talks a lot and with great force as if he were giving out the last word on the subject. Greer said of him, "His domineering is due to the fact that he is a captain in the army reserve and goes to army camp in the summer. Army training destroys tact, I think. Also his training in mathematics makes him think that all problems are easy to solve, that you can handle people like numbers." It is true, however, that Keller is dominating only to those subordinate to him either occupationally or socially. He is extremely domineering with teachers, for instance, but is considered a most likable quiet fellow by upper-middle class and lower-upper class people.

Teachers generally dislike Keller. They claim he is inconsistent, ordering one thing one day and taking it back the next. He gathers teachers together in meetings and lectures them but does not discuss their problems. He is accused of asking the opinion of teachers about other teachers. He bullies teachers by dismissing their ideas with gruff and definite countersuggestions, and teachers say of him that he takes their ideas, puts them into practice, and takes all the credit. Greer is extremely antagonistic to Keller on this score. "I get tired giving him ideas for which he takes all the credit." Mr. Greer is, of course, sensitive about his personal status, and this is deepened when he helps the superintendent and knows that because of his academic deficiencies he cannot aspire to be superintendent.

Mr. Keller is, however, conscious of the attitude of the teachers. One day he said:

> Before I came here the teachers never met before school opened and they made quite a kick about meeting, but now I think they are all resigned to it. The trouble is that there are certain individuals who feel that I am persecuting them personally, rather than just trying to establish some system. I have always been brought up to look upon the fact that the central organization is running the show and to take orders even though I disagree with them sometimes, but here it is very difficult because these people have been going for so many years and have never had any of that sort of control.

This comment demonstrates not only differences in the characters of Greer and Keller, but the differences necessary in approaching different kinds of people. Greer is an expert in having good relationships with the lower classes and hence does not "high-hat" them. Keller, on the other hand, is dependent upon his relationship with the upper-middle class. He finds that emphasis on the intricacies of a job and the special aptitudes required for it appeals to the upper-middle class person. This attitude caused considerable trouble for Mr. Keller. Although the Board of Education was predominantly upper-middle class or higher, the mayor was lower-middle class. He was an ex-officio member of the Board of Education and in this capacity as well as that of mayor he disliked Keller and was always fighting him. This dispute was clearly a dispute between the lower three and the upper three social classes. The mayor did not like "fancy doo-dads in the schools," and Keller did not make things easier for himself by discussing in professional terms the problems of education.

In time the mayor was able to force Keller out of Yankee City. This happened because Keller had not become thoroughly entrenched with the upper-middle and upper-class people.

I thought when I was getting this job that it was a step up and that it really was an advance, but I really found that it wasn't. I can't go away for a day or so without somebody saying that this guy was taking his salary and not earning it, not doing any work. I've had no opportunity to make contacts of the kind that I want. I've met very few people, in fact I have had no opportunity to broaden myself; I have been confined to this job.

In reference to clubs and associations, he said:

I never was much of a joiner. When I came here people told me that I ought to collect several high-grade fraternal orders and join them for what they could do for me, but I didn't do that. In the first place, I like my home life and am very much interested in it, and I don't like going down to one of these clubs and playing pool or billiards or bowling or anything like that. My schoolwork carries on through the day and doesn't stop at five o'clock the way a lot of jobs do.

Without belonging to powerful groups, including both upper-middle and upper-class groups and groups which include all social classes, Keller could never count on strong enough community support to back up any of his proposals or dicta. Keller was made superintendent of schools because he was a good football coach and the football fans knew him, although of course he qualified academically for the job. But he could not receive support for his educational programs on the same basis. He should have won the support of a new and powerful group on the basis of his educational policies or his social class position.

Mr. Greer, the senior principal, has the task of mediating between the upper-middle class Board of Education and lower-class people who send their children to his school. He does this successfully because he owes allegiance to no one save himself. He lives out of town and has few intimate social relationships in Yankee City. He even eats his lunches alone. "I live out in the country and bring my own lunch. I wouldn't live in town for anything because I might become too identified with some group.

I wouldn't be able to see the problems objectively." Greer wants personal success, a not uncommon trait, especially for a person who is abnormally small in physical stature. His frustrated social ambitions are channeled off into success in his professional and economic life. Greer believes that there are in the lower classes many children who could rise in the world and do well. After all, he himself has risen. He stresses individualization because that means that there will be some chance given to the better minds to get ahead. On the other hand, he does not believe that "getting ahead in the world" comes solely through education. These beliefs reflect Greer's own experience, and they are most acceptable to the lower-class people of Yankee City, if not to the upper three classes who tend to believe that "background" and "breeding" are necessary prerequisites for success. Greer is not a lower-class person, and he cannot find intimate relationships in the lower class. His attitudes are not in keeping with upper-middle class attitudes, so he stays out of the middle-class social life of the community as much as possible, which aids his success as principal of a predominantly lower-class school.

Keller, on the other hand, is unsuccessful because he does not participate adequately in any part of the community. His job is to put into effect policies set forth by the upper-middle class Board of Education for the whole population. Especially should he look out for the middle- and upper-class students. He practically hands over to Greer his responsibilities to the lower-class people. He hands over to the high-school principal many of the problems concerning the social education of the various classes of people. He should, however, be in a position to cope with the lower-middle class politicians, such as the mayor, but he is not because he has no group to back him up. To be a successful superintendent of schools in Yankee City not only must one have some knowledge and skill in running a school system but one must be a good upper-middle class politician. Keller is too aggressive, too domineering and too aloof to be accepted by a strong group of people, and so he has a difficult time. Where Greer's lack of interest in social mobility stood him in good stead, Keller's ineptitude at social mobility caused him to fail at his job.

THE SCHOOL BOARD

Behind the educational administrator stands a group of citizens who are responsible for the property and operation of the educational institutions and represent the public in matters of educational policy. These representatives, members of school boards and boards of trustees, must see to it that the educational system serves its social functions.

School boards are usually elected by the people, though in certain cities they are appointed by the elected head of the municipal government. In Old City, Hometown, and Yankee City, school boards are elected. Table XII shows the social composition of these three school boards.

TABLE XII

SOCIAL CLASS COMPOSITION OF SCHOOL BOARDS

	Old City	Hometown	Yankee City
Upper upper	..	..	1
Lower upper	..	2	1
Upper middle	5	3	5
Lower middle	..	..	1
Upper lower	..	..	..
Lower lower	..	..	..

A number of studies of the social composition of boards of education agree in finding that school board members are predominantly business and professional men.[1] In towns and cities, about 75 per cent of school board members belong to these two categories. Farmers make up the bulk of rural school boards.

In a few cities organized labor is active in school board elections and often elects a representative who is active in labor union affairs. Labor union members who are elected to the school board are usually lower-middle in status. Occasionally organized labor succeeds in electing a full slate, or at least a majority of the board. In such cases, the pro-labor members are usually not labor union members but middle-class professional and business people. The public educational policies of organized labor are and have been essentially middle-class in nature. Their aim has been to provide for a maximum of social mobility through education.

Boards of trustees of colleges and universities are upper-middle class, or higher. Probably no board of trustees contains more than a small fraction of people of lower-middle status when measured on a national scale. The upper-upper and lower-upper classes furnish the majority of trustees and regents for state universities and for most endowed institutions. However, there is a liberal sprinkling of upper-middle class people on nearly all college boards. The exclusive colleges have their fates resting securely in the hands of upper-upper class people, with the upper-middle and lower-upper classes furnishing a vital stream of new blood.

CHAPTER X

The Negro in the American Caste System

THE AMERICAN CASTE SYSTEM

SINCE Emancipation the Negro has tried to use the school to gain equality. His struggle for education has greatly benefited him, but he has not succeeded in his quest. In fact, the school often functions to keep him down rather than lift him. At times the school has been an effective weapon in the Negro's hands, but its skillful employment by his opponents through the years has helped block his social advancement. In the South, with rigid caste controls, distinction between Negro and white education is formal, legislated for, and universally recognized. There are always separate schools for whites and for Negroes. In the North, informal and less rigid controls frequently achieve similar results.

Caste, we said earlier, is like class inasmuch as it places people in social strata with unequal distribution of the privileges, obligations, and duties society offers. Caste is decidedly different from class because it forbids marriage outside the caste level and insists on endogamy. Caste also forbids social mobility. Success stories do not fit the caste structure. None of the stories told in the chapter on social mobility could be found in a highly organized caste society, for caste prohibits and punishes this kind of behavior. When the study was made in the Deep South, three hierarchies which crosscut the society were found. They were a white class system, which we have described, a Negro class system, which was like the white one, and a caste system. We shall describe and analyze the third hierarchy, for it is necessary for us to know how it operates in the lives of people if we are to understand how education operates among American Negroes. The system existing in the Deep South is found in various forms wherever there are Negroes in the United States. The Deep South has it most systematically organized.

The Negro is placed in an inferior and subordinate position

through a great variety of white ideas and behavior which are all interrelated. He is considered mentally inferior and incapable of learning what the superior white group learns. These beliefs are held despite the scientific evidence to the contrary. He is said to be biologically inferior and a "lower form of organism." He is therefore animal-like and his behavior is thought to be emotionally undeveloped. This makes him more primitive in his behavior and obviously inferior to whites. Many of the religious say that these inherent differences were placed there by the will of God. This whole attitude is well-expressed by a white doctor, who said:

> The way I look at it is this way: God didn't put the different races here to all mix and mingle so you wouldn't know them apart. He put them here as separate races and He meant for them to stay that way. I don't say He put the Caucasians here to rule the world or anything like that. I don't say He put them here to be the superior race; but since they have a superior intellect and intelligence, I don't think God would want them to mingle with inferior races and lose that superiority. You know the Negro race is inferior mentally, everyone knows that, and I don't think God meant for a superior race like the whites to blend with an inferior race and become mediocre. I think God put all the different races here for a purpose, the Negro and the Indian and the Chinese, and all of them, and He didn't mean for them to mix. I think I am right in saying that, and my attitude is Christian-like.[1]

The Negro is believed to be childlike and as such in need of the superior hand of someone who will be responsible for him and guide him as a parent would a child. A white person in the Deep South spoke for most of the group when he said:

> They are very much like children; they have no thought for the future and only think of their immediate wants. They are really just like children. They can't be left to themselves; they don't have the ability to get along. They really need white people to direct them.[2]

The whites feel that the Negro is unclean. This feeling about the Negro's uncleanliness is much like that found in India. The uncleanliness is not so much physical as spiritual. It is an emotion that is often very powerful. Whites often refuse to eat or drink from a dish that has been used by a Negro or to buy a garment that has been tried on by a Negro customer. On the other hand, whites enjoy having their meals cooked and dishes washed by Negroes.

The attitudes and feelings are organized by an elaborate set of rules and a code of etiquette. The rules and etiquette serve to keep whites and Negroes socially and physically separated, to deprive the Negro of his rights and advantages under American democratic law, and to give the white man more than his share of the available things which people want. We will itemize a few of them.

In the United States an average of $80 a year is spent on each child's education. In ten southern states, $49 is spent on a white's education and $17 on a Negro's.[3] In Mississippi and Georgia only $9 is expended on a Negro child's education. White people in America have a life expectancy of sixty-two years, while Negroes have but fifty-one years. The present rate is a decided improvement over what it was a generation ago. The Negro's low life expectancy is directly related to his inability to get the kind of medical care and health protection that is available in America for whites. In the United States, North or South, the Negro is first fired and last hired. In many industries he receives smaller pay than a white man for the same job. He is systematically excluded from many jobs; many unions will not permit him to join, which keeps him out of occupations where management often willingly would employ him. In many states of the Union the Negroes cannot vote or hold office. The total effect of this system of deprivation is to put the Negro at the bottom of our social system. These items of deprivation are separately stated, but they are parts of a larger whole—the American caste system.

The Negro is kept in his lowly place by the refusal to permit him to climb out of this position through the rule of "once a Negro always a Negro." This is the basic rule of caste everywhere. A man may educate himself, develop a brilliant professional career, acquire wealth and property, and behave with all the nicety of a southern aristocrat, but he is still a "nigger" in his caste status. Should he try to marry outside his own group into a white one he would be physically punished and possibly lynched. The rules of caste forbid mobility and prohibit marriage above his level.

It is in the social context of caste that we must look for our understanding of Negro education in the United States. It is no accident that Katherine Green was forced to live among white people. She was *with* but not *of* them. The other children and their parents could look forward to marriage with childhood playmates or others like them. She could not. Joe Sienkowitz could dream about a time when as a great violinist he might return to

Hometown and be received in the homes of the Peabodys and the Browns and possibly even marry one of them. She could not. Her life and the lives of all her people are outside that of the white groups.

THE NEGRO CLASS ORDER

Five social strata may be distinguished in the Negro community of Old City: an upper class, two divisions of the middle class, and two lower classes. In studying the Negro community in Old City it was found that the following traits of individuals or families are the most important bases for clique and social class relationships: the recognized social position of parents; amount of educational achievement; skin color and hair form; church and associational membership; talent; manners and dress; condition and type of house and furnishing.

The members of a social class themselves recognize that the fundamental test of their class status is their ability to participate regularly in the social life of certain other persons. In the colored society, for example, the expression "class *with*" is used to mean "able to go around with" (socially). One middle-class person will say of another: "Joe can't class with the big folks [upper class]— he goes around with the people right here in Turnersville [middle-class neighborhood] just like the rest of us."

In the sense in which a social class is here conceived, therefore, its membership can be identified empirically upon the basis of either of two types of information: (1) records of *common participation of individuals in noneconomic groups,* such as churches, associations, clubs, large dances, teas, picnics, weddings and funerals; and (2) the verbal expression by individuals of their *willingness to associate with other persons in these social relationships.*

The most explicit and detailed expressions concerning class status were made by persons at the top of the colored class structure of Old City. These upper-class persons stated that there were three social classes. They knew and identified the members of the upper class and the highest ranking individuals of the middle class. They also stated their conception of the social traits and techniques by which these individuals had achieved high social status. All the upper-class informants emphasized the weakness, however, of class sanctions.

The colored upper class is divided into two groups: (1) a socially withdrawn group which seems to be essentially fixated upon being white and (2) a socially active group which sometimes attempts to compensate for its not being white by being free in its emotional and sensual expression.

There is no doubt that in the Deep South, as in most colored societies, the chief "weakness" of the class structure lies in the relative lack of economic stratification within the lower caste. As a direct result of caste taboos, for example, colored persons are excluded from all white-collar and professional occupations, except in the few colored businesses or educational institutions. Physicians, dentists, and lawyers, moreover, are relatively few in colored, as compared with white, societies in the South.

The caste system as enforced by the southern state legislatures makes no provision for the education of colored physicians, dentists, or lawyers;[4] and colored people are systematically excluded from white-collar work in business and government. The relative lack of economic or occupational differentiation within colored societies is fundamentally the result of educational deprivation and lack of economic opportunity. Although the operation of the economic system permits a few colored persons to achieve high occupational status, it does not permit a sufficient spread of occupations to allow the development of an occupational hierarchy. In all modern Western class systems, on the other hand, occupational status and economic status are highly correlated with class status. Occupational and economic status may have been acquired from one's ancestors, or be largely honorific, as in the case of upper-class families who have lost their wealth but have preserved the reputation of wealth and of high occupational status in the past. In any historical view of class, however, there seems no doubt that economic stratification would prove the most nearly constant factor.

NEGRO AND WHITE ATTITUDES TO NEGRO EDUCATION

The attitude of Negroes in Old City to education varies in accordance with whether one is making evaluations on the basis of the whole "caste" or on the basis of the social class system within the caste. Education, some Negroes say, will do the most to raise the position of the Negro in American society. Education, say a few others (mostly upper-class), just makes lower-class Negroes dissatisfied.

Leaders in the colored community frequently spoke of the high rate of emigration among the educated children of colored farm owners during the preceding thirty years. A leading colored businessman, commenting on the emigration of all eleven children of a colored farmer, who had once been successful, agreed with the landlords that the education of colored people made them unwilling to stay in Old County. The interviewer asked, "Well, how do you account for the fact that the Durant children didn't stay? He has a fine farm, you say."

Yes, but Durant's children were all educated. He educated them all, and that made them unwilling to stay on the farm. They wanted to leave, as soon as he'd educated them.

[Bitterly] This other man's sons aren't educated, you see. They are more or less ignorant. You know that's why these white people are against educating these Negroes. They say: "Educate a nigguh an' you ruin him for the farm." And they're absolutely right, too! As soon as they get a little education, they're simply not going to stay on these farms. The white man knows that, and that's why he won't give these Negroes good schools!

Or more directly we can hear a Negro upper-class man say:

I don't believe education, I mean compulsory education, is doing this country any good. I told a fellow once, who was state senator from around here, that compulsory education was a dangerous thing, a dangerous thing. Because as soon as you take a country boy and teach him something about the world and give him new ideas, you ruin him for the farm. And you make a Negro dissatisfied with his position. As long as you keep him ignorant, he's satisfied to work for some white man on the plantation, but as soon as he learns to want other things, he comes to the city to try to get them. When he gets here, he finds the white man has everything, and he can't get the kind of work or job he wants, and he is dissatisfied. And then you have a dangerous situation. "If you want to keep your present civilization, you've got to keep the poor people ignorant," I said to this man. And it's true. If you educate people and then try to treat them the same as if they weren't educated, you've got trouble on your hands. A man who's got nothing at all sees you or somebody else with everything and he's dissatisfied. You can't blame them, either. In our present civilization, a few people have everything, and all the rest have nothing. Of course, I believe democracy is the only fair system of government myself. I really do.

On the other hand, we hear another Negro upper-class man talking at the opening of a new school. He spoke on the necessity of education for Negroes and emphasized the point that parents must not take their children from school just because they are old enough to help with the work, but that the parents must struggle and sacrifice to let the children go as far as they possibly can in school. He also said that the people of the community must make an effort to keep their school open eight months out of every year —even though the county provided for only four months' schooling.

The main speaker, a Negro college professor, at this school opening began his speech by saying,

Once I was a great believer in Negro education—preached it all the time —but now I doubt whether it's good or not. You educate your children— then watcha gonna do? You got any jobs for 'em? You got any business for 'em to go into? Well, if you haven't, do you think they gonna be content to come back to live in a li'l one-room house wid no 'lectric lights—wid no comforts? No, education changed their tastes. They don' wanna wear overalls, they gotta have better things than you got—an' why? Jes' 'cause they got education and learned about things—got themselves usta' things you don' even know about. Yeh, that's what education does! If you can't give 'em those things—and they ain't got jobs, what they gonna do to get 'em? They're gonna be crim'nals, bootleggers, robbers—is that right? Yug, that's right, you know it.

A Negro lower-middle class man who runs a shoe repair shop says,

You know, there's jus' two things Negroes need to get up all ovuh the worl', jus' two things. They need capital and they need education. When they get those two things, they'll be all right. They need all the education they can get.

The white attitude to Negro education is somewhat similarly divided. The white superintendent of schools said, "The South has made a mistake in ignoring and neglecting the better class of Negroes. There should be more of them in the schools as they are the ones who can and will influence the Negroes in the right way. We should never have made the mistake of trying to keep the Negroes down by force and not giving them the proper education."

When asked if there was any sentiment against a high-school education for Negroes, he said, "The better-class whites seem to have no feeling against it. I do sometimes get complaints against some such thing as teaching Latin to the Negroes; some feel that it would be better to give them something more practical. I am a believer in Latin but the modern tendency is, and probably rightly so, to give things of more practical value but which are also good for their educational value such as history, civics, commercial courses and things like that."

The white woman who supervises schools in Old County said, "Not all Negroes are capable of getting an education. So many of these 'burr-heads' can never learn very much and all they want is to have a little cabin and raise cotton. They are at a very low stage of development, and they are perfectly content to live in a cabin with cracks in the wall and a leaky roof."

Many landlords and some members of the county school boards were opposed to the development of more efficient schools for rural colored children. They expressed the fear that the providing of even a thorough grammar-school education for colored students would make them unwilling to remain on the plantation and would end by depleting the supply of workers. Equally important in many cases was the belief that educated colored people were less amenable to the caste sanctions, less deferential, submissive, and dependent, and therefore a danger to the efficient working of the caste system. Several instances of the refusal of a literate tenant to accept the landlord's settlement of his accounts and the subsequent dispossession of such a tenant were reported. The rate of emigration of those children of colored farmers who had received advanced education, furthermore, appeared to be much higher than for the similar group among whites. For example, the educated children of six of the largest colored farm owners in Old County emigrated between 1933 and 1935, and their parents were compelled to follow.

The attitudes of whites to Negro education contain these propositions: (1) they ought to be educated to do things better and so that "they can lead their people in the right way" and (2) "You can't teach them much anyway and besides they ought not to have too much education or they become 'uppity.' "

There is, then, a fourfold conflict of attitudes toward education for Negroes in Old City and Old County. Within the Negro caste we see the attitudes that (1) "education will save the race" contrasted with the attitude of some of the upper-class Negroes that (2) "education for the better class of Negro is a good thing." From the white caste we get the attitude that (3) Negroes will be better workers if educated contrasted with the attitude that (4) too much education makes the Negroes dissatisfied. The result of these conflicts is a school system dependent on whites for basic financing (enough for Negro education) and educational control and dependent on Negroes for supplementary financing and community interest.

The superintendent of schools in Old City, when interviewed by a white fieldworker, comments thus on the Negro schools:

I will have to admit that they aren't as good as the white schools, but I think you will find they are generally better than any of the other Negro schools in the state.[5] We have so many Negroes here it is quite a problem. However, we have a very good high-school building and they go up through the twelfth grade. If it was actually compared to the white school it would only be about the same as tenth or eleventh in the white school.

The Old County white school superintendent, when asked by a white interviewer how she managed the Negro schools, says:

I try to encourage them to run the schools themselves with my assistance. I appoint the teachers but try to hire those whom the patrons of the school prefer. They have three trustees for each school who are elected by the school patrons and if they tell me they want a certain teacher I will appoint the one they want. Of course, every teacher must have a state certificate and I see that they are the proper sort and will attend to their job and not rat on it. The trustees are expected to look after things at the school and see that the teacher is on her job. I find it is better to as far as possible let them run the school themselves and select the teachers; it is better to give them a teacher they like even if she is not quite as well qualified as some other they don't want. If you put in one they don't like and who can't get along with the community they will make it hot for her.

The most visible difference between educational facilities for whites and Negroes is the actual school building and equipment. In Old County, for instance, many schools were in reality churches.

When asked about the schools meeting in the churches or in buildings adjoining churches, the superintendent just quoted said:

There are several in the county that meet in churches. I think the origin of that custom came about before I came here when the county arranged to help the Negroes build buildings which would serve as both church and school. I don't know about other counties but I know that they built a number of churches under that arrangement here. Then the Negroes are great on lodges and many of the buildings near the churches are lodge buildings which are used for school.

When asked about the maintenance of the Negro schools and if the Negroes help keep up the buildings, she said:

The county is supposed to keep them up but of course we don't do it as well as we should. The last three years especially we haven't done a thing to them. I do try to encourage the Negroes to help keep up the schools; they give picnics and benefits for the school and raise a little money. No matter how little it is I encourage them and tell them it is a good start. Sometimes they will come to me and say they have raised $5 or $2 and I encourage them to keep it up. Not that it amounts to so much, but I think they must learn to do things for themselves. Besides they have more of a feeling that it is theirs and they have a part in it. They should always be helped to do things for themselves and not merely be dependent on others. I find that they get along much better if I let them handle their own affairs as far as possible rather than for me to go tell them to do this and not do that. They must work things out for themselves, of course with my help when needed, and not just wait to be told what to do.

THE NEGROES GET A HIGH SCHOOL

The story of how the Negro high school in Old City was built is an interesting illustration of the conflicting attitudes toward Negro education. The following story is told by the superintendent of schools:

That was started sometime about 1925 and a separate bond issue was voted just for the building of the Negro high school. We used as our propaganda to the people the fact that the old Negro school was in very bad condition and had been condemned as a firetrap and was also entirely inadequate for nearly a thousand students who were using it. We ran a series of ads, paid for by businessmen around town, putting it before the people and stirring up sentiment in favor of the bond issue. We also used this approach, that most of the businessmen here made their money by skinning the Negroes and if there weren't any Negroes to skin they just wouldn't make a living. (They were emigrating to the North.) Then we talked to a lot of the leading businessmen, contractors; they generally agreed that the educated Negroes made better workers, and we used that idea. The businessmen and all the leading people in Old City are generally well-disposed toward the Negroes and many of us take the stand, not openly, but it is understood, that it is impossible continually to subordinate any race or group of men without resulting in serious conditions. One of the most important elements was the fact that the leading Negroes also were lending their influence. The Negro school principal then was highly respected in the white community, he was almost white, and he had lots of friends and influence. Then Dr. Dupres and other leading Negroes lent their aid. In a way the bond issue was really a tribute of respect to the leading Negroes of the community.

It was an independent bond issue and carried something like four or five to one. Another thing we did was to ask those Negroes who were eligible to vote not to do it so it was purely a matter of the whites voting for this bond issue.

When it was remarked that it was unusual to get money for a Negro school directly he said, "I think this is the only case in the state where a Negro school has been built without having to attach the appropriation to some white school issue."

The version of the leading upper-class Negro man was as follows:

I don't think I did so bad when I picked the site for that school, do you? You know the old school was a firetrap. The place had seventeen stoves— one in each room. Then the steps were all rotten, and most of the wood-work. So I took pictures of the steps and the interior and sent letters to all the leading white organizations in town, describing the condition of the school. The principal, who was my best friend, was a timid man, and he was afraid for me to ask for repairs and an annex. But I went to the Board of Education and told them, "That school is a regular firetrap. The steps are all rotting, and it's dangerous for these children to go there." I showed them the pictures I had too. Well, I asked them for $10,000 to repair the old school and for $40,000 to build an annex. The principal thought that was too much. He said, "You have to be careful with these white people." I think he was afraid he'd be blamed and lose his job, if there was any agitation for a new school. But I was independent financially and had nothing to lose.

You know they decided to give us a new school. I persuaded them by appealing to the white man's pride and vanity. The old school was in a neighborhood that had become white. So I said to them, "You don't want these Negroes going to school there. Give them a new school and put it in a neighborhood where they'll all be together." Of course, they fell for that. They let me choose the site. They wanted to float a bond issue for $90,000, but they knew they couldn't get that past the voters, without a rider, so they made it $75,000, and it passed without any rider. These people voted for it three to one!

Then we started a strong P.T.A. at that time. My wife raised $1,500 one time for furnishings for the school and $1,000 another time. We turned $2,500 over to the superintendent. My wife still has the cancelled check for the $1,500 she raised. We bought most of the desks in that school and furnished the Home Economics Department.

On looking back at what was going on at the time the Negro high school was built, it is safe to say that the whites were anxious to make some concession to Negroes because so many of the young ones were emigrating to the North where there were better opportunities.

There are two schools for Negroes in Old City, a small elementary school and a larger combined elementary and high school. There are about 1,400 pupils in the schools and about forty graduate from high school every year. There are twenty-three teachers in the two schools—of whom seven are upper-class and the rest upper-middle. There is a single curriculum which is academic— more so than the curriculum in the white high school. There is little vocational training. Although the building is relatively new, there is little up-to-date equipment in the school—the community

through the Parent-Teacher Association is supposed to provide this equipment.

Of fifty students who were known to have gone on to college and university, all were in the top two classes. Some college education is almost essential now to be upper-class, and those who are upper-middle class but mobile upward go on to college. Most of those who go on to college do not complete work for a degree with the exception of those who go to professional schools such as medical schools.

The main job of the schools at present is to teach "the three R's."

The census of 1930 reported that 29.9 per cent of the colored people in Old County and 26.9 per cent of those in Rural County were illiterate. The figures had been practically the same ten years before (32.0 and 33.8 per cent). The fieldworkers' experience convinced them, however, that at least half the rural colored population of Old County and a higher proportion in Rural County were illiterate and that most of the adults who were "literate" had only had enough training to enable them to read their names and to calculate the value of their cotton.[6]

For most of the lower-class Negroes to become literate is the important thing. This also satisfies the white people, for this makes the Negro efficient as a worker without making him effective in any competitive trade or job. This does not suit the upper- and upper-middle class Negroes who want much more from education. It is these people who are the driving force behind the P.T.A. and any other movements to improve the school and what it is doing.

Class and the P.T.A.

The class dynamics of associations in Old City were most vividly illustrated by the history of the Parent-Teacher Association of one of the Negro schools. In the course of five years this organization, started by an upper-class clique, decreased in size until it included only the dominant upper-class clique and less than a dozen other members, all from the upper-middle class. This branch of the P.T.A. had been organized by the most influential Negro upper-class woman in Old City at the suggestion of the white superintendent of schools. It was conceived by the white superintendent as an organization to raise funds for the equipment of the Negro school. Since the white school board did not equip the Negro high school with a science laboratory, a playground, or seats for the study hall, the upper and upper-middle Negroes in Old City sought to raise funds for this equipment.

By the device of holding the meetings of the newly formed P.T.A. in churches, where it could draw upon the large lower and lower-middle classes for economic support, the upper-class leaders of the association raised $1,500 at one time for the purchase of land, and $1,000 at another time for the purchase of equipment. This money was turned over to the Negro school principal, who diverted part of it to other uses, and agreed with the white superintendent to use the remainder to buy science equipment, valued at less than $500. It is not known whether the white superintendent and board also diverted a large part of this fund. All that is known is that at least $2,500 was raised by the P.T.A. and that less than $500 worth of equipment was purchased. In spite of the disorganization and loss of membership resulting from the misuse of these funds, the upper social clique in the P.T.A. continued to raise money for the equipment of the playground, for the equipment and staffing of a school cafeteria, a piano, a Rosenwald library, the equipment of the Home Economics Department, and so on.

Nevertheless, this branch of the P.T.A. was never successful in integrating the parents of the thousand pupils in the school into the organization. From the beginning, the control of the association was entirely in the hands of the upper and upper-middle clique, who were effective in raising money but not in relating the great mass of low-status Negroes to the teachers or to the school. The teachers were also upper and upper-middle class; the result was that the P.T.A. was a rigidly class-typed organization, which failed to include the parents of 99 per cent of the children. This curious organization, with officers and no members, had pursued its class-bound policies from the beginning. Its founder, whose upper-class prestige and efficiency in obtaining white donors made her a successful money-raiser, stated that she had chosen her leaders only from the top social group among the parents.

I organized each classroom into four teams, each of which was to be responsible for raising $20. Then I personally went to see as many parents as possible in each schoolroom and picked out the five most influential to head the teams. Over these five I put one general captain, one of the biggest women in town. And I'm telling you, in little or no time, we had our $1,500. Why, the first meeting after the drive began, I had $900 in cash put on my dining-room table.

By the fifth year, this policy of choosing leaders had so antagonized the parents in the other social classes that only the officers and teachers attended P.T.A. meetings. The number of people present at the monthly meetings never exceeded twelve, of whom not more than four had children enrolled in the school. The work of the association was still entirely limited to money-raising chiefly for the school cafeteria.[7]

The social class dynamics underlying the shrinkage of P.T.A. membership had become clear even to the association's leaders by the fifth year, when parents of only four of the thousand pupils in the school attended meetings. In this period, the most influential upper-class Negro man in Old City stated at a P.T.A. meeting that he felt the present members and teachers should co-operate in making "an appeal to all parents of all the children." He then went on to point out the class factors in the association's inefficiency as follows:

We want to interest the parents who really need guidance and assistance in bringing up their children, who don't know the meaning of making good citizens—and it's our duty to get in touch with them. We who are here tonight and who make a point of attending every meeting of the P.T.A.— we aren't the ones who really need so much the services which the P.T.A. can render—we want to help raise the masses. Now I would be very glad if some plans could be formulated whereby the P.T.A. could get in touch and work with every parent.

He was also aware that invidious distinctions between the clothes and other status symbols of the upper and lower groups kept many lower-class parents away.

We know that our parents frequently have to work out all day. They're tired when they get home—lots of them don't have the kind of clothes they'd like to wear out—and stay home on that account. But through personal visits from the teachers, they can be made to realize that those aren't the things that count. What counts is their support and their presence.

A second officer of the association, who made a canvass of the city in an effort to interest parents in the meetings, reported that antagonism to the social status of the officers was evidently strong. She discovered that the P.T.A. at the smaller Negro elementary school in Old City had a large active membership and a high degree of co-operation between teachers and parents. Class analysis of this group by the fieldworkers revealed that the officers and the teachers in this branch were chiefly lower-middle class people and that they had the support of a large group of lower-middle and lower-class parents. Attendance at meetings ranged from fifty to a hundred parents, although there were fewer than five hundred pupils in the school. At a money-raising program held by this low-status P.T.A. at a small Negro church, more than two hundred people were present. Of these, almost half were men, an unusually large proportion for any meeting in Old City.

The relative effectiveness of these two branches of the P.T.A. in organizing parental support for school programs must be understood in terms of the social class goals of the dominant groups in the two organizations. In the one, both officers and teachers were upper and upper-middle individuals with secure high status, who had no prestige-gain to make through the organization of the great mass of lower-middle and lower-class parents. In the other, both officers and teachers were lower-middle class who increased their prestige in their local community and obtained social mobility within the class system by organizing school-community relationships. The class values and antagonisms which prevent effective leadership by high-status individuals in such an organization are illustrated by the comments of an officer of the P.T.A. branch first mentioned. In referring to the leadership of the second P.T.A. group, she said:

> They are the washwomen and the scrubwomen—the ignorant people who haven't anything to give—who are their leaders.

The teachers are poorly paid and one of the P.T.A.'s functions is getting money for the teachers. Much of the money raised by the P.T.A. is used to supplement the teachers' salaries rather than to buy equipment. Some criticism is heard of this, but it is the only way the teachers can live. One Negro woman said, "The white school teachers don't get paid less than $100 a month and they have a law saying they aren't to have more than thirty children in a class—our poor teachers have fifty or sixty children in a class and the highest gets $55. Besides they have to buy all their own supplies out of that." Actually salaries range from $40 to $54 a month except for the two principals, who get about $85 a month. Salaries are paid only during the school term.

The wife of the school principal said that unless she had her garden it would be impossible for her family to live on their income.

> As it is we have to do without a lot of things that we need. With three children, I should have three quarts of milk a day but cannot afford it. I make all my own and the children's clothes, but still can have just one decent dress at a time. If I had more time, I would do some outside sewing but by the time I finish a day's work, I am really ready to rest.
> I am able to raise enough vegetables to provide the family with all the fresh vegetables from early spring up to late fall—and during that time I can enough to last during the winter. I also raise some chickens.

This school principal was making $90 a month when he first came to Old City, but his salary was cut 10 per cent. This is paid only during the school term. He paid $15 a month for rent, $22.50 when light and heat were included.

His wife says further that she does not know how the teachers manage to live at all, their salaries are so low.

> It's a shame what they pay colored teachers down here and make them work twice as hard as white teachers. But you see they gotta pay the white teachers enough so they can pay some colored person to cook and wash and iron and clean for them. But the colored teachers don't need anybody to do their work—they're supposed to get up early and get their breakfast and fix their dinners and wash out what clothes they need; then go to school and teach and come home and finish up! Keep 'em busy so they won't feel they're getting too far up in the world. That's why they won't pay colored teachers anywhere near a decent salary in the South.

The economic factor is most important to any consideration of the education of Negroes in the South. We find such comments as this from teachers:

> On rainy days only seven or eight children in my room come to school. Same in other grades. The children have no rubbers or coats or shoes to withstand rain.
> It snowed yesterday (six or seven inches) and not one child came to my room out of 110 enrolled. Other grades had four to eight children. The high school had only children of economically high parents. There were only five students in high school study hall.
> Next day only four of 110 in first grade came to school. If they had any shoes or coats to withstand the weather they would come, because school is warm and I know their cabins are around forty degrees to 50 degrees on a day like this. One girl told me today that snow blew into her house through cracks all day yesterday.

When the upper-class community leader was asked what he thought the average income per month of Negro families in Old City was he said $24. Few men earn more than $9 or $10 a week and then few of the jobs allow them a full month's work. The women earn about $10 or $12 a month.

When asked how they managed to live on such small money incomes he said he didn't know. "Some clothes and food they get from 'white folks'—then for the rest, they live largely on credit, frequently not paying their bills."

A fieldworker accompanied a social worker who was distributing tickets for the "Poor Children's Christmas Tree" and notes: "About forty homes were visited—most of these merely one room—the furniture varied from one in which there were an elaborate bedroom set and dinette set (chairs and table) to nothing but a bed and a few boxes and a table in the barest."

The schools for Negroes in Old City have at least three functions: (1) to educate the children in terms of literacy; (2) to subordinate Negroes to the white, superordinate caste; and (3) to provide a prime focal point for Negro community integration.

The children are taught primarily to be literate, to read and write and figure. They are taught history and some science and Latin if they stay in school long enough. They are taught little along vocational lines inasmuch as the expected occupation for most of them is that of labor, servant, or cotton farmer. Social classes are largely economic divisions in this Negro community. There are laborers and servants, a few merchants and businessmen, and a small number of professional men. These three socio-economic levels correspond roughly to three levels of educational achievement ranging from simply "some schooling" through high school graduation to college and university training.

The most obvious way in which the Negroes are subordinated through the schools is economic. The whites control public funds, as the Negroes are for all useful purposes disfranchised in the South, and facilities for adequate Negro education are not provided. This results in several interdependent ways of subordinating the Negro. By curtailing facilities Negroes are not taught a trade or settled vocation so that they will not be able to compete with whites for the jobs requiring special training. As much as possible the Negro is kept in the common laborer class. Whenever the Negroes want something for their schools they must either beg for funds among themselves (thus setting them apart from the white community) or beg from the white school authorities from whom they sometimes receive a small sum. This makes the Negroes feel grateful for the kind things done for them, thus adding to the subordination. For instance, at one of the money-raising affairs the chairman introduced a white man: "Mr. King, one of the colored folks' good friends, has been good enough to come to the meeting and has been such a liberal contributor, we would be very glad to hear whatever he might wish to say."

He replied briefly. "We're very glad to be hyah tonight and we sartney enjoyed the program you all had. I'm glad to see this here schoolhouse 'n I hope it's gonna be a success— 'n' it will be if we jes keep on a-co-operating."

Much applause and one old woman, evidently an employee of the Kings, who had induced him to come to the meeting, shouted out, "I sho luv mah whut folks!" at which everybody laughed.

Or we might visit the county superintendent of schools on payday. Here we would see that the superintendent calls the colored teachers by their first names. The teachers are made to stand—they are never allowed to sit down in this office. They are made to line up around the desk but there the superintendent tells them, "Don't come too near, stand back away from me." Then comes a speech such as this one: "Now I want you all to teach these colored children not to be lazy; make 'em work!" As a matter of fact it is quite unnecessary that these rural school-teachers come all the way into town for their checks, but the superintendent makes them come after their money instead of mailing it.

We might be reminded too that when the new Negro high school was being contemplated and the bonds issued, the Negro leaders were asked not to take any part in it because the white people wanted to do something for the Negroes. By depriving the Negroes of adequate educational facilities and by contributing only a minimum of educational opportunity, the whites constantly subordinate the Negroes.

In contrast to the use of the school system by whites to subordinate Negroes, the schools provide a focal point of community interest for the Negroes. Education is frequently considered to be the one thing that will best improve the lot of the Negro and consequently there is a good deal of community interest in education. Then, too, the more dominant Negroes are interested in getting a good education for their children so that they may go on to professional jobs. Added to this is the fact that one of the more generally available jobs is that of teacher, so that improving the schools has direct benefits for the upper-middle and upper classes. It is for these reasons that we find the upper-class leaders of the community, their families, and friends so busy in the money-raising campaigns for the schools. A rather obscure aspect of this function of the schools as a focal point of community action is that through the community interest in the schools some of the aggression against whites, resulting from oppression, can be expressed. This is possible because of the sacredness of education in the total American culture. Demands can be made and things can be said in the name or interest of education which could not otherwise be expressed freely. The same is true of religion.

One can talk of "race improvement through proper education" in Old City without arousing the antagonism of whites which would result, for instance, were one to talk about "race improvement through political action."

The schools for Negroes function in opposite ways; they are used by whites to subordinate Negroes, on the one hand, and used by Negroes to improve their position and attack "white oppression," on the other.

THE NEGRO'S RIGHT TO DEMOCRATIC EDUCATION

Being at the bottom of our social system, the Negro provides a crucial test of how far we Americans are willing to put into practice our belief in the right of everyone to an education. The treatment he receives in our public schools tells us whether we provide equal opportunity for everyone or only for white children in this country. At the present time most American Negroes are systematically deprived of the chances ordinarily offered white children. Edwin R. Embree, in his book *The American Negro, a Handbook*, reports: "The annual expenditure per pupil in 1935-1936 based on a careful survey of ten [southern] states was $17.04 for Negro children and $49.30 for white children. Judged by dollars and cents alone in these states the white child has three times the advantage of the Negro child. In other states the difference is not quite so great, but in all of them the prejudice which subordinates and prevents most lower-class whites from learning is greatly increased and intensified when applied to the Negro. It was no accident that Katherine Green was the girl who walked alone. The barrier of tradition effectively taught Katherine her role and separated her from whites."

Forced into subordinate minorities after arrival in America, the European immigrants have used the school as the principal institution to get equality for themselves and their children. The American theory of the melting pot has given them strong encouragement. The cultural traits possessed by the immigrants have become symbols of lowly social status, but through the melting pot these symbols can be changed and everyone can become a good American. The theory of the melting pot does not work for the Negro. (Even the Red Cross felt somehow that Negro blood was not quite the same or as good as white blood, and that the two should not be mixed.) In the case of the immigrant the symbols which he learned in his ethnic homeland with some effort can be unlearned here, and the more highly valued American ones substituted. Because of this fact, the school has become important in raising the social levels of ethnics and contributing to the gradual elimination of lowly evaluated cultural groups. The symbols of the Negro's social inferiority are unfortunately physical, and these physical *traits* he must keep; they can only be re-evaluated as *symbols*. The school cannot help him as it has the immigrant, for his problem is different. If American education could have functioned for the Negro as it did for our ethnic groups, the Negroes as variant people would have long since disappeared from American life.

It is the duty of the school to teach the whites the knowledge we have gained through the sciences about the mental equality of all races; it should teach everyone that the present social inferiority of the Negro is the result of long-continued systematic subordination. The Negro child must be given the same opportunity to acquire an education and fit himself for life as the white child receives. The talented Negro must receive the same encouragement and advancement that we have insisted should be given the talented white. If this means the use of federal funds and federal supervision, then the federal government must take this responsibility.

The battle for occupational, financial, and status equality for the Negro must be fought on other fronts, for this fight is not the responsibility of the school. Industrial management must learn that the talented Negro who has been well-equipped in school should be given the same opportunity for advancement and security of position as his white competitor. Labor organizations must protect the rights of both Negroes and whites. These and other goals must be won before the Negro obtains equality, but the school should not fight these battles. It should struggle to give the Negro equal opportunity to learn, and it should teach whites the truth about racial equality.

CHAPTER XI

Who Shall Be Educated?

Making Education Work for Democracy

It is now time to draw a few generalizations which will provide us with a set of principles on which we shall then build our recommendations. In reaching these conclusions and in suggesting a program of action we are guided by democratic values. We have asked ourselves how democratic values may be better realized in the lives of Americans through education, always taking into account the facts of the social organization of our country.

To make democracy work in our complex modern society it is essential that a high order of technical-and civic competence exist at all social levels. Teaching such skills—technical, as well as social —is increasingly the responsibility of the schools. The individuals who exercise these skills should be the products of a superior native capacity, trained by highly competent instructors, and so placed after training that they can adequately employ their abilities. Wherever individuals with ability of one kind or another are found the schools must recognize their native endowments, train them, and reward them. To do less invites filling critical positions in governmental and private organizations with incompetents who do not possess the skills necessary to do their jobs. Malfunctioning of the democratic order because of mere technical inadequacies is an important factor in arousing a questioning attitude toward democracy as a way of life; and indeed, if democracy is incapable of recruiting and training properly qualified people to do its work, there is strong reason for such skepticism.

Previous chapters have provided ample proof that the present method of screening the able from those of less ability is not satisfactory. Some of the children in our lower social levels are endowed with high capacities. At present many of these children leave school early, discouraged by disappointing experiences and lack of recognition. They quit before receiving the training which would permit them to contribute their best to our life. This is personally frustrating to them and socially wasteful. A new system of selection and encouragement must be developed which will keep these children in school and allow them to compete with those above them on the social ladder. To do its job this selective system must operate at all social levels; it must be particularly adapted to the lower ones, for most of our people are in them.

If America is to maintain its democratic way of life, a larger number of people with ability must function competently in all parts of our life. We must use fully all our human resources if we are to have the necessary personnel to administer efficiently the work that society must have done.

There is enough native ability in America to provide the skilled individuals who are needed to solve our problems. It is demonstrable that some of the ills of the present are directly traceable to our failure to use trained people. Because of our status system we have maintained many people of inferior ability and training in responsible jobs who should have been eliminated to permit competent people to rise from lower levels to fill these higher places. We must spread our net wider to find people of talent wherever they exist and we must permit them to compete with everyone for the prized positions. The rewards of talent and hard work must be made more secure and more sure.

The job of social engineering which will give efficient form to what we propose will demand more than mere mechanical changes. The educational problem is moral as well as technical. The American schools must recognize this fact. There must be a basic core of moral experience incorporated in curricula to equip sub-adults with codes which will permit them to act with moral understanding of themselves and others and make them feel their responsibility to society. America as the "Promised Land" has become a symbol of privileges and rights to its citizens and immigrants. "What's in it for me?" and "What can I get out of it?" are guiding principles of too many people who educate themselves like a burglar preparing for a safe robbery by acquiring sharp and powerful tools to crack the bank of opportunity.

Until our schools allow all our children to learn their responsibilities and obligations to themselves and others and until our professional schools recognize the necessity of indoctrinating their pupils with codes of ethics to guide professional practice we will continue turning out moral imbeciles who are as incapable of doing their jobs as the technical incompetents. It is imperative that when we recruit young men and women for high positions character as well as ability be made of prime importance. Until it becomes clear to young people as they progress through our schools and colleges that good character has its own rewards there will continue to be more emphasis on privilege and less on duty in their thinking about their life careers. The school is not, however, the only institution which could be used to improve democratic living. All other American institutions, such as the church, government, and associations, must assume their full share of responsibility.

As long as we have our present social structure education must be adapted to it or we will produce a generation or more of maladjusted children and unhappy adults. The school in America, whether we like it or not, must function to make democracy work in a status system that is only partially equalitarian. Only as our social order changes can the school indoctrinate its pupils with economic and political philosophies of human relationship which are now in sharp conflict with the prevailing social system. The thesis of some educators that American schools should be the instruments of propaganda for a particular type of economic or political thought is wrong and must be discouraged. Although the guiding philosophy of such propagandists may be democratic, the methods advanced are unreal and dangerous. Propaganda education that conflicts with the prevailing mores produces conflict in the lives of those taught and does not provide growing children with a realistic orientation to the social world in which they must compete for a living and for status.

In a complex society in which education must take account of social change and prepare youth for it, teaching does not mean indoctrination for specific and set traditional goals. Most of our present belief in hard and fast rules of democracy and our assumption that the present or any other social order is immutable and eternal are dangerous precepts to pass on to those who grow up in a changing world. The school must educate for enough flexibility in the student's outlook to encourage him to expect social change and to help him direct it and accommodate it to his own and other people's lives as the occasion demands. This is but another way of saying that education must fit reasonably well

into the prevailing social structure—in this case a changing one—
or result in maladjustment of children.

When first confronted with the fact of a class order in our
country many Americans feel compelled by their sentiments to
disbelieve the evidence and minimize its significance. The indoctrination of childhood is too strong for objective weighing of
facts so that they can arrive at sound conclusions. Other people
do accept the fact of unequal status as true and demand complete
abolition of our status structure and the substitution of pure
democracy. Once again democratic fictions acquired in early
training betray their efforts to think clearly, for it is impossible
to wipe out our status structure. Those who hold that economic
reorganization is desirable are fond of saying that if all economic
differences between people were destroyed and the means of
production were communally owned by the group this would
result in equality for all and a pure democracy. They are mis-
taken. It is true that unequal distribution of economic goods and
the private control of the means of production are powerful and
necessary factors in the maintenance of our *present form* of class
order. Were they abolished, radical reorganization of the *form* of
our status system would inevitably occur. But it is equally sure
that pure democracy could not be born through such a change
and it is certain that it would not produce an equalitarian status
system. When Soviet Russia abolished the capitalistic, czaristic
regime it destroyed one form of rank but immediately substituted
a new one through use of such forms of rank as the party
hierarchy, the differential evaluation of occupations, and the
superior and inferior military orders within the Red army and
navy.

Any country with a huge heterogeneous population, with many
cultures, many regional variations, and countless world-wide affiliations must have a series of hierarchies which organize power
and prestige within the social structure if order is to be maintained.
To integrate all of the several groups in a factory it is necessary
for a hierarchy of control to be established. This is many times
more true for a large country, since not one but many hierarchies
are necessary if the work of the community is to continue. Social
equivalence of corresponding positions among the many hierarchies is recognized: for example, in Russia men of top status in
the army and of similar position in the diplomatic corps, the school
system, and the economic order, as well as the higher ranking

artists, tend to be classed together in a superior general rank, as opposed to those in each of these hierarchies who are at the bottom. The latter tend to be classed as belonging to an inferior group. This produces higher and lower social levels of the class type. At present the Russian hierarchies permit greater mobility, have less social distance from top to bottom, and provide fewer mechanisms for individuals or families to maintain high social status. There is greater emphasis on rewarding the individual and his family with prestige for services rendered to society than in the United States.

The purely equalitarian state is a luxury enjoyed by only the most simple and primitive groups because their populations are small enough and their problems of sufficient simplicity to permit it. The decision to be made by those who disapprove of our present inequality and who wish to change it is not between a system of inequality and equality; the choice is among various systems of rank. Efforts to achieve democratic living by abolishing the social system are utopian and not realistic. The remedy for the present ills is certainly not to try to abolish the whole existing structure. It would be impossible to destroy most of our major status differences without violent revolution. There are few who would go this far. Most people want to maintain some form of the present structure. To be practical those who favor drastic change must accept some type of hierarchy as a substitute for the present one. The rest of us must recognize the general fact of hierarchy, and we must work out a procedure which will make our hierarchical system best serve democratic values.

With the recognition of these facts it is now possible to continue our discussion of educating Americans for democratic living. Some kind of elite is present in any complex society. A highly trained and intelligent elite will serve society best when rewarded by positions of esteem and privilege. The Russians, with all their strong belief in equality and in the individual being rewarded by making a contribution to society, have not hesitated to reward with positions of power and prestige those who serve their country.*

* Mr. Wendell Willkie's account in *One World* of his conversation with the superintendent of a big airplane factory in Russia clearly illustrates this point. Willkie says the superintendent "lived in a comfortable house much better than the average, and in peacetime had an automobile."

"How does your pay as superintendent of this factory compare with the average skilled worker in the plant?" I asked him.

It seems probable that most of the members of the Russian elite, when motivated by powerful family sentiments, would want their children to have the same positions in society as their parents. These sentiments are basic in our family structure. For them to change, our present-day family organization in civilized countries would have to change. The demand by those who reach places of prestige and power that their children keep the social place of the parents is the real problem of hierarchy in democracy. The question arises to what extent children should retain positions of prestige earned by their parents. Our answer is that such positions should be passed on from parents to children with reasonable assurance, but that the competition from below should be such that a large proportion of these jobs would be yielded to the socially mobile from lower positions. In other words, those from the bottom should be given more than a fighting chance to compete with those above them. The children of parents in superior positions should not be penalized because they have been fortunate enough to have been born to such parents, but it should not be assumed that they can inherit the right to continue in the same positions. To advocate less flexibility would mean a closed class order where no one could rise; to advocate more would lead to complete change of position in each generation, which would violate some of the sentiments that dominate all men and would lead to social chaos.

If such a system were adopted, fewer of the unfit who inherit opportunities to get the education necessary to maintain them-

---

He thought for a moment: "It's about ten times as much."

That would be on the same ratio twenty-five or thirty thousand dollars a year in America, and actually was about what a man of similar responsibility in America would receive.

The Russian continues talking to Willkie: "With my first savings we bought ourselves a nice house," he told me.

"And then?"

"Then we bought a place in the country, where the family could go for vacation and I could go for a rest, or to fish and hunt when I could get away from the factory."

"And now that you have these things all paid for, what do you do with your extra money?"

"Oh, I keep it in cash, or put it in government bonds."

"But who will take care of you when you are an old man?"

"I'll have some cash put aside, and if I don't have enough, the government will provide for me."

(Wendell L. Willkie, *One World*, Simon and Schuster, 1943, Paper-backed Edition, pp. 27 28.)

selves in high positions would succeed, for the competition from some of those rising from below who were more able and just as well trained would defeat them. There would be greater turnover in the acceptance and distribution of positions than we now have but the transfer would be regulated and ordered. Consequently, there would be an increase in the use of available talent and the encouragement of those trained for all forms of life. In any society like ours there is room for only a few at the top. The saying "There is plenty of room at the top" is fiction in any society which is not expanding rapidly. Therefore, in America the concept of competition must be rephrased, for our society is no longer expanding rapidly. The belief that everyone who can should aim for the top means frustration for many and unnecessary defeat in the lives of those who with less ambitious aims could have achieved a satisfying success. We believe Americans should recognize and reward less ambitious but socially important goals. We believe the top should be widened as much as possible and should be open to all, but we believe that it should be stressed and made explicit to everyone that the number of people with qualifications for these top goals is quite small. It should be also stressed that there are other worth-while goals and that the country respects those who occupy them.

All of us—parents, young people, and teachers—need to understand the fact of social mobility more clearly. It is an important part of our American tradition and should remain, but it should be better understood. We need to understand that the goal of those who are rising in our society is social as well as economic. We need to see more clearly that various subgroups in our society can aim at different goals and that it is not necessary for everyone to shoot for the top. With this clear view of social mobility we could adopt more explicit methods of recognizing and encouraging ambition in talented individuals. The school seems clearly to be the instrument best suited for making social mobility a better understood and more clearly defined activity.

Together with providing for the upward movement of individuals who deserve to rise in our social system, we should provide for some flattening of the social pyramid by improving our system of distributing goods and services. It is clear that the economic level of the lower classes must be raised. This does not mean that we can abolish the lower levels of our society. It only means that individuals of the lower strata will get more of the things people want and deserve. It is now not only morally desirable but also technically possible to raise the economic level of the lower group, since our present technology is capable of producing all that is needed and wanted by everyone. Yet we have many people who are not getting the basic necessities for existence. The last two wars have demonstrated that our technology when given the proper stimulus can produce beyond anything dreamed of in previous times. Instead of modifying our system of distribution to produce a more satisfying social adaptation for everyone, we have insisted on clinging to an economy that was developed for a discarded technology, an economy that is inadequate and incapable of producing enough for everyone.

If our way of life is to be maintained we must modify our economic structure sufficiently to permit the full social use of our technological system. As long as we were technically incapable of producing an adequate income for everyone the philosophy of scarcity which still permeates our society was adaptive, moral, and realistic. Today we know we have the technical skill to produce enough to satisfy the needs of everyone. The problem is social, not technical. Our democratic social order will not continue to tolerate such a state of affairs. When scarcity was necessary, we could demand only what was then possible. Now that abundance is possible, democratic morality must insist upon and obtain an economic order that will produce and distribute enough to satisfy the needs of everyone. Until these changes are reached we will continue to be an unsettled and disunited people.

The Hard Facts

Education must serve democratic purposes. Education must give all boys and girls their chance. The educational system must select and encourage those with the best abilities wherever they are found. Education must promote social solidarity through providing equal opportunity, through freeing people from narrow class prejudice and snobbery, and through teaching the kind of morality that democracy requires.

In making education serve democratic purposes, the educator faces many difficult problems. These problems are caused by certain irreducible stubborn facts about human beings and about our society. These are the hard facts:

CHILDREN ARE NOT BORN EQUAL

We no longer believe, if we ever did, that all children are created equal biologically. Children are born equal in America only in the sight of God and the law. This means that they have equal spiritual claims to consideration as individual human beings, and that they have equal rights in the law courts. In no other important sense are they born equal. We know that children are born with diverse potentialities. We believe that, even if all children had identical social and physical environments, they would grow up to be different in ability, personality and physique.

We also know that children with talent or unusual ability are born to parents of low as well as high status. Everybody knows that dull, ordinary, and superior children are produced by parents of high social status. Everybody also knows that parents of low social status may produce superior children.

We know that children are not created equal socially. Every individual is born into a set of social positions. A child is born into a social status by sex. From the day of its birth a boy child is treated in a different manner from a girl child. A child is born into a status by his birth order in the family. The first-born will receive different treatment from those who come later. The last child will get a special kind of treatment. A child is born into a status by his family's position in the social structure. The child of the house "on the hill" will have nurses, servants, tutors. He will grow accustomed to having people treat him with deference. He will develop manners and speech that mark him as having grown up "on the hill." The child of the house by the railroad tracks will grow up with entirely different manners and attitudes and expectations in life. A child is born into a status by his nationality or race. If he is Jewish, Italian, Irish, German, Chinese, Hindu, Negro, he will undergo the treatment accorded to people of his group, treatment which varies from one part of the world to another and from one time to another.

These social inequalities quickly become part of the person. They get into his nervous system. They engender habits and attitudes which mark him as a person and over which he has little conscious control. The marks of social status appear in a person almost as soon as the genes which he inherits from his parents' bodies display themselves in observable characteristics, and it becomes impossible to tell how much of the person is due to heredity and how much to environment.

By the time children are five or six years of age, they are such a diverse lot that equality of opportunity for them obviously is not identity of opportunity. To treat them all alike would be like putting little chicks, ducklings, baby swans, puppies, kittens, and bear cubs all in a pond together and waiting to see how they respond to this "equal opportunity."

ONLY A LIMITED NUMBER OF PEOPLE CAN BE ACCOMMODATED IN THE UPPER SOCIAL AND ECONOMIC LEVELS OF OUR SOCIETY

The fact that the educational system is a system of elections for positions of higher social and economic status makes it advisable to gear the selecting machinery to the demand and to the capacity of the social structure. If too few people are selected and promoted through the educational system, the upper levels will be filled through other agencies and perhaps not filled with people as well equipped by skill and training for the positions. If too many people are selected and pushed up through the educational system, competition will become fierce for the higher-level jobs, and some people will have to take positions below the level for which they have been trained. Doctors will have to take jobs as laboratory technicians, engineers as factory workers, and teachers as clerks. This will cause feelings of dissatisfaction with the social order, and the social structure may be strained beyond its tolerance limit.

To get an idea of the relation of the output of our educational system to the demand and to the capacity of the upper socio-economic levels of our society, we shall turn to the census. About 4 per cent of our male workers are classified as professional workers. Certainly the great majority of the professional workers are college trained. About 9 per cent of male workers are classified as wholesale and retail dealers, proprietors, managers, and officials, omitting farm owners. At present only a small minority of the wholesale and retail dealers, proprietors, managers, and officials are college graduates. But we are building up a belief in this country that a college education is a good preparation for a business career, and consequently it may be reasonable to suppose that a third to a half of the jobs in this second category are acceptable positions for college graduates. The remainder of the male workers in this category hold positions as owners or managers of small retail stores and similar jobs not usually thought of as positions for college graduates. Consequently, it seems reasonable to suppose that the boys who now graduate from college, constituting about 7 per cent of their age group, can find suitable places. The crop of graduates probably contains a few more than can easily be placed but the surplus serves the twofold purpose of providing competition and thus keeping the income of professional workers down to competitive levels and of providing educated leaders for social reform movements.

A little more than 3 per cent of the adult female population in the age range 21-64 are classified as professional workers. These are mostly schoolteachers, and the majority of them are not college graduates. But a college degree is now being required for most new women teachers. In view of this fact, and in view of the further facts that many women marry soon after graduating from college and many others marry and drop their employment after only a few years of professional work, it appears that the 7 per cent of women who now graduate from college can find satisfactory places in the social structure. Still, there has been during the past decade an oversupply of women teachers in some sections of the country, principally the cities. And a good many women college graduates have gone into secretarial and clerical occupations.

Thus the educational system seems to be sifting out and promoting approximately the right number of people for the positions in our society that are considered proper positions for college graduates. Whether the system is also selecting the best people for these positions is a question we cannot answer so readily.

But what of those who are not promoted? There are many young people who start on the path toward college graduation but never reach the goal. About half the students who enter high school take a college preparatory course, and no more than one in three of this group of "college preparatory" students actually enters a college. Less than half of those who enter college finish a college course. Thus the high school and college operate crudely as selective agencies by admitting about six times as many students to the college preparatory course as actually finish college work. All these boys and girls expect to become doctors, lawyers, teachers, engineers, chemists, editors, bankers, accountants, business and industrial executives, or they expect to marry such people. The high school either tolerates or actually encourages their belief in the myth that there is plenty of room at the top of the social structure for all of them.

One important qualification should be made with respect to the generalization that only a limited number of people can be accommodated in the upper social and economic levels of our society. While the number is limited, it is not fixed at the number we have in our society today. The proportion of doctors, teachers, and other professionals who serve other people might increase greatly if more money were spent on health service, education, and other social services. Thus, the number of positions in the upper half of society might be increased considerably. But even if this number were doubled or tripled, the number would still be limited to a small fraction of the total adult population, and many young people in our society would be disappointed in their efforts to achieve these positions.

ECONOMIC MOBILITY IS PROBABLY DECREASING

However efficient and fair the educational system may be in performing the selective function, it is only one of the factors affecting economic mobility in our society. If the other factors are such as to decrease the numbers of people who rise or fall in the economic scale, education may become more and more an agency to train children to occupy the economic positions of their parents. It is important, therefore, to know what the trend is in respect to economic mobility. Is economic mobility increasing, remaining constant, or decreasing?

Such facts as we have, and they are not conclusive, indicate that economic mobility probably is decreasing in this country. That is, a smaller proportion of poor boys is becoming wealthy. Wealth and economic power are retained more within families and within the group that is already high in the economic scale.

The most useful study bearing on this question has been made by Taussig and Joslyn. These men, working at the Harvard Graduate School of Business Administration, sent questionnaires to the fifteen thousand leading businessmen of the country asking them for information about their family, their education, how they got started in business, and so forth. They found that "the present generation of American business leaders has been recruited in greater part from the sons of business men, and only to a minor extent from the sons of farmers and manual laborers."[1] To investigate the trend of economic mobility, they placed the busi ness leaders in age groups and then classified them according to their fathers' occupations. Thus it was possible to compare the fathers' occupations of the older business leaders with the fathers' occupations of the younger business leaders. The data are shown in Table XIII.

TABLE XIII[2]

FATHERS' OCCUPATION OF BUSINESS LEADERS CLASSIFIED ACCORDING TO
PRESENT AGES

Occupation of Father	Present Ages of Business Leaders						
	Age 35-39	Age 40-44	Age 45-49	Age 50-54	Age 55-59	Age 60-64	Age 65-69
Laborer—Unskilled or Semiskilled	2.6	2.3	2.7	1.6	2.3	2.3	2.2
Laborer—Skilled	7.4	8.6	9.0	8.7	9.5	9.8	8.4
Farmer	7.5	10.0	12.2	12.9	13.5	16.3	17.0
Clerk or Salesman	5.7	6.3	6.1	6.0	5.7	3.1	3.7
Minor Executive	8.0	8.9	7.6	6.3	6.6	6.3	4.9
Owner Small Business	18.2	17.8	19.1	20.6	20.7	20.4	22.4
Major Executive	23.5	19.0	16.0	17.9	13.7	13.0	12.4
Owner Large Business	14.4	14.7	13.8	13.5	15.7	15.0	16.0
Professional	12.7	12.4	13.5	12.5	12.3	13.8	13.0
Totals	100.0	100.0	100.0	100.0	100.0	100.0	100.0

This evidence on the trend of economic mobility is slender. It indicates, at any rate, that economic mobility is not as great as many would like to believe and that economic mobility may be decreasing. The educational system is thus faced with the task of promoting economic mobility in a society whose structure is such that economic mobility is not increasing.

SUCH ECONOMIC MOBILITY AS NOW EXISTS IS LARGELY RESULTANT
FROM THE LOW BIRTH RATE OF PEOPLE IN THE UPPER
SOCIO-ECONOMIC GROUPS

Such economic mobility as now exists in our society is made possible largely by the fact that people in the upper classes do not have enough children to replace themselves. The students of population have discovered that people in the professional and managerial classes fall short by 20 per cent of reproducing their numbers. That is, every five such people in one generation will produce only four in the following generation.[3] If we should assume that all the children of upper and upper-middle class parents manage to retain or to better these positions (an assumption which is, of course, not true), there would still be opportunity for people from below to rise and fill one in five of the upper and upper-middle class positions. This is a rather limited opportunity, since one-fifth of the upper and upper-middle positions is only 2 or 3 per cent of the total number of positions in our society and all of the lower and lower-middle classes, some 85 or 90 per cent of the population, may be candidates for these few higher positions.

Still, this factor making for socio-economic mobility is undoubtedly one of the most significant factors in our social organization. Farmers have the most children, working people in the towns and cities are next, and professional and managerial people have the fewest children. Children of farmers and working-class people are needed to fill in the ranks of the upper classes.

An article in the *Princeton Alumni Weekly* entitled "The Vanishing Race of Princetonians"[4] declares that the average number of children per Princeton graduate is 1.6, while an average of 2.3 children would be necessary to replace this group.

In Hometown, the Peabodys have only one child, and most of their friends have only one or two children. If Kenneth succeeds in retaining an upper-class position, he will have as companions some boys who have come up from below him. The Browns have three children, which is about the right number to keep their numbers constant, because some of the men and women of their class will not marry. Many of the Browns' friends have only one or two children. Tom Brown or some of his friends may grow up to positions of upper-class status along with Kenneth Peabody. The Sienkowitzes have five children, as do a number of poor but industrious Hometown families with English, Irish, Swedish, and German names. Some of the children of these families will push up into the middle class. Even the Jones family, with so many children that the teachers have lost count, may produce one or more youngsters who miraculously show ambition, industry, and intelligence, and climb up into the more respectable levels of society. The entire process of pushing up from below is made easier by the disposition of the Peabodys and some of the friends of the Browns to have few children.

In some European countries, the upper classes are as fertile as the lower classes. This is true in Sweden. And it may become true in this country. In such an event, the amount of economic mobility will in all probability be still further lowered.

ECONOMIC IMPROVEMENT IS WIDELY IDENTIFIED WITH MORAL IMPROVEMENT

We have seen that a number of factors conspire to limit economic mobility to a few and probably to fewer people than formerly were able to rise. Yet the imperative "Thou shalt rise" is as vital in the minds of middle-twentieth century boys and girls as it was in the minds of their forerunners in the nineteenth century. It is the mark of a good citizen, a good provider for his family, a good American, to leave his children better off than he was left by his father.

An elderly doctor in Hometown was speaking to his adult son about saving money. "When I was your age," he was saying, "I had saved up the nucleus of the inheritance which will go to you and the other children." "Father," the son replied, "you have already given us the best part of our inheritance—our character, ambition, intelligence, and education. We can get along very well without inheriting money. I hope I can pass on to my children as good an inheritance as I have received, but I do not desire to leave them much money." The father replied seriously, "I could not face my Maker unless I knew that I had left more money to my children than I started with."

Economic increase is identified with moral improvement by a large middle section of our society. The professional man or small businessman wants to build up a small fortune, hoping to establish his sons and daughters more comfortably in life than he has lived. The clerical worker, the farmer, and the mechanic will slave to give their children a college education which means an "easier time" in life. The unskilled laborer often denies himself comforts and even necessities in order to send his boys and girls through high school so that they may start higher on the ladder than he will ever reach. All these people face their fellow citizens with feelings of pride and assurance of approval at thus pushing their children upward. This is a large part of their morality.

Often the labor-union member, proud as he is of his union card, does all he can to prepare his children for a position with management or to promote them into a profession. It seems as if there is something immoral about earning one's bread by the sweat of one's brow for two successive generations. The children catch the notion quickly and often come to feel guilty if they do not justify their parents' hopes and sacrifices by rising in the economic scale. The young man or young woman who will deliberately cast in his lot with the laboring class, in spite of superior education, is a rare person, looked at with some suspicion and mistrust by his fellow workers as well as by his friends and relatives.

To be sure, there is more than a moral imperative driving the lower-class man to improve the economic status of his children. There are the real insecurity and anxiety of being dependent for food and shelter upon the upswing of the business cycle, with intermittent periods of poverty and unemployment.

FAILURE TO RISE IN THE SOCIAL SCALE AND CONSEQUENT FRUSTRATION ARE INEVITABLE FOR MANY

In this world where upward mobility is the hallmark of "good citizenship" and success in life, but where the possibility of upward mobility is not so great as social myth leads people to believe, many boys and girls are destined to failure. Of the 580 boys and girls in a thousand who reach the third year of high school, about half are taking a course which leads to college. One hundred and fifty enter college, and 70 graduate. These are average figures for the country as a whole. With variations in various parts of the country, an average of some two hundred out of every thousand young people fail to achieve the goal toward which they started in high school. Thwarted ambition and frustrated hope result. Doubtless many accept the reality easily enough and settle into a niche in life without bitter feelings. But certainly many others develop resentful feelings toward society in general and toward their more fortunate fellows in particular. If they fail to rise in some other ways than through education, they become centers of disaffection, and society loses some of its necessary solidarity.

Girls have the desire to rise and they feel the frustration of failure to rise as much as, or more than, boys do. The evidence is clear that women are more conscious of social mobility than men. For girls there are two ways of climbing—by marriage or by exercise of talent. School teaching has long been the principal avenue of rising by exercise of talent. Virginia Crane is one of the many who have followed this road. With other professional and business positions becoming increasingly available to women, it appears that opportunity for social mobility of women is increasing. But by far the greater portion of girls must achieve higher status by marriage if they achieve it at all. A girl takes a college preparatory course in high school and goes on to college and usually marries a boy who, she hopes, will "get somewhere." If she marries a boy who doesn't "make the grade," she must give up hope of joining certain women's clubs, of having servants in her home, and of climbing higher in the hierarchy of women's affairs than her mother and her girlhood acquaintances. Since the number of boys who can achieve social mobility is so limited, many ambitious girls will be disappointed by what seems to them to be failure on the part of their husbands.

Social Mobility and Social Solidarity

All these facts tend to show that upward social mobility is a scarce article and all the more valuable in the eyes of many people because of its scarcity. They also tend to show that the school system has severe limitations as a social elevator. Its capacity is limited, and it is not free.

Nevertheless, the American school and college system is the greatest agency we have for equalizing opportunity and for promoting the rise of able young people. Through it we maintain a degree of social mobility probably greater than that to be found in any other country.

The educational system promotes social solidarity, or social cohesion, partly through its provisions for social mobility. A society has social solidarity when its members believe that they have a substantial common ground of interest—that they gain more than they lose by sticking together and maintaining intact their political and social institutions. A certain amount of social mobility seems necessary to maintain social cohesion in our class-structured society. The possibility of rising in the social scale in order to secure a larger share of the privileges of the society makes people willing to "stick together" and "play the game" as long as they believe it gives them a fair deal. Yet social mobility must be limited if it is to be valuable. A large measure of it would spell revolution or social chaos.

Thus it appears that social solidarity in a society like that of America is fostered by social mobility if the latter is kept within limits. Too little social mobility would give rise to widespread dissatisfaction and to attempts to change the social order by violence. Too much social rise and fall would produce a chaotic society in which few would care to co-operate socially with others because the rewards would be so fleeting.

Educators, therefore, should try to adjust the educational system so that it produces a degree and kind of social mobility that is within the limits which will keep the society healthy and alive. But here is where they face a dilemma. They are under constant pressure to educate too many to rise in the economic scale. The American people, believing in a myth of unlimited social mobility, send their children to high school and college as speedways to place and power. If the educators attempt to regulate traffic, they are accused of being undemocratic, and they may lose the confidence of the public. Yet there is clear evidence that our educational system is now permitting too many to use high school and college for the purpose of attaining unavailable professional and managerial positions, with resultant failure and frustration and loss of social solidarity.

PROPOSED EDUCATIONAL PROGRAM

We have seen how our educational system is related to social mobility and to social solidarity which in turn are related to the health of our society. We have reached some conclusions about the role that education should play in improving our democracy. We come now to the application of these ideas.

What do these conclusions mean when applied to the educational system? What do they mean for the organization and administration of the educational system and for the content of the educational program? Looking toward the future improvement of education, what do they mean for the selection and preparation of teachers? We shall make a number of positive proposals in answer to these questions.

Content of the Educational Program

The first six or eight years of schooling should have a common content for all. In the common elementary school American boys and girls should assimilate the literature, history, and biography that will bind them together with a common background of tradition and emotional experience. The democratic values should be experienced and related to the affairs of everyday life. Holidays should be celebrated—both the national holidays, such as Washington's Birthday and Thanksgiving, and socictal holidays, such as

Christmas and Easter.[5] Thus the common loyalties of Americans should be inculcated along with the common skills of communication which are always taught in the elementary school.

The American school system does all these things fairly well. Present practice in these matters is, on the whole, good practice. Occasionally, however, an effort to improve the teaching of the fundamental skills conflicts with the teaching of fundamental loyalties and values. Tendencies toward segregation of pupils for more efficient teaching of the fundamental skills should be examined carefully to see that they do not threaten the teaching of the common loyalties.

The secondary school should continue the elementary school program with a common core of "education for the common life" occupying a third to a half of the school day. English, social studies, fine and industrial arts, and to a limited extent the mathematics and science of the high-school curriculum belong in this common core. The secondary school should teach our democratic values—belief in the dignity and worth of every human being, co-operation for the common good of all, tolerance, freedom of speech, freedom of worship. Educators could do no better than to imitate the superior practices of certain schools observed by the Educational Policies Commission and described in the book *Learning the Ways of Democracy*.[6]

This program should extend through the high school, and it might be carried through the junior college or the first two years of four-year colleges. The experiments in general education which have been made during the past decade in many secondary schools and colleges are all useful in exploring for the type of program which is needed. The questions to be asked about this program are: Does it inculcate common democratic values? Does it give young people of all social statuses a feeling of common cultural heritage? Does it provide equally well for boys and girls of all social statuses and all kinds of intellectual ability?

A part of this common program should deal with the basic social problems and social issues of our society. It should aim to teach an approach to social problems which all American citizens can adopt and which will help them to deal with their inevitable clashes of economic interest in ways which will maintain co-operation among the various social and economic groups in the nation. It should teach students techniques of study, reliable sources of information, and methods of conducting discussion that will prepare them for the continuing study of contemporary problems, which is a responsibility of an intelligent citizen.

Another feature of education for the common life should be socially valuable work experience. Every boy and girl, regardless of social position, should work with others on projects designed to raise the common standard of living. This work should not be paid for. It should be the free gift that every potential citizen makes toward raising the entire societal standard of living.

This period of work service might come at any time between the ages of twelve and twenty. Under American conditions, it might be wise to make work service a part of the early high-school program. At about the age of fourteen or fifteen every boy and girl might spend an hour or two a day working on a project that will make a concrete improvement in the standard of living of his community and from which he will profit along with all others in his community. In a community like Hometown such projects might be organized as: clearing land for a park, building a swimming pool, cleaning up alleys and vacant lots, caring for a community forest.

Through this program of education for the common life Tom Brown and Bob Jones and Katherine Green will have the experience of working together for something that is valuable to them all and something that is bigger and more important to the larger society than the interests of their own families or their own particular sections of the community. They will also learn to celebrate the same heroes and holidays. And they will learn to employ intelligent democratic methods for solving the social problems about which they will have genuine differences of interest in later years.

But Tom Brown and Bob Jones and Joe Sienkowitz cannot have all of their education in common. Somewhere there must be a differentiation in terms of their vocational goals. In America the high school contributes to the vocational preparation of most students. Bob Jones is almost sure to drop out before he reaches high school. Tom and Joe will probably go on, but they must pursue different courses toward different occupational goals. Consequently, a part of the educational program must be differentiated. Those who are going from high school to a job should be taking courses which will prepare them for their work. Those who are going into homemaking should take some courses which will prepare them better for the business of operating a home.

Parallel with the common program of general education for all there should be a program of vocational preparation to which every high-school student devotes a part of his time. The student who expects to go on to college and to become an engineer, or scientist, or teacher of mathematics should study mathematics in a rigorous preprofessional course. There should also be preprofessional courses in physics, chemistry, foreign language, and possibly in other areas. Thus the college preparatory curriculum would be recognized for what it is—a vocational course.

Vocational preparation in high school or college should not be derided as "materialistic." Lifework is important in every society where people have to work for a living. Choice of a lifework and preparation for it are most important tasks of young people. They are clearly recognized as such by young people themselves. The high school and college are institutions for vocational training, and rightly so, in our society. When trigonometry and French are recognized as vocational courses just as auto mechanics and shorthand are, instead of being set up as "cultural," it will be easier to do the job of guiding high-school students into those courses which will best meet their needs.

The high school and the junior college should develop more terminal vocational courses. A terminal vocational course is a course that comes at the end of formal education and trains directly for a job. It is a good general principle that the last formal education of a boy should be vocational—should lead straight toward a job. The same principle applies to girls if we recognize homemaking as a job and the homemaking program as vocational. The high school, which provides the last formal education for seven out of ten of its graduates, should provide a broader program of terminal vocational courses. Among other things, a type of apprenticeship program should be established which helps students to get started on the ordinary jobs of a small community like Hometown—clerking in stores, truck driving, working in a garage or service station, working in a restaurant, and working in an office.

The high-school program should have a third element in addition to the general education and the vocational training already mentioned. There should be a wide variety of avocational activities —intellectual, artistic, mechanical, and social—in order to provide opportunities for all sorts of boys and girls to excel. These should be linked with adult activities in the community. There should be literary activities leading into the adult literary activities of the community, artistic and musical activities leading in a similar manner to adult artistic and musical activities. There should be exhibitions of craftsmanship and gardening, flower-raising and stock-breeding, to show all kinds of youth ways of excelling which they can carry into adult life. Joe Sienkowitz should have an opportunity to get into musical activities that will bring him recognition throughout the community. If he does not succeed in becoming a professional musician, he still may attain a desirable status in Hometown as a local musician, even though he takes a low-paying position in a factory office. Tom Brown or one of his social status may make a hobby of gardening. As he grows up in Hometown he may become an ordinary middle-class businessman like his father, but his gardening ability will give him a certain prestige that will class him with the Peabodys, who pride themselves on their garden.

The avocational or extracurricular program of the high school would thus help to provide many different kinds of prestige pyramids in the school and community so that practically every person could work up to a point near the top of at least one pyramid and thus gain satisfaction denied him if he strove and failed to get to the top of the socio-economic pyramid.

Organization of the Educational Program

The educational system should be organized to recognize superior abilities wherever they are found, to reward them, and to train them. This is what we mean by equality of educational opportunity. Equal opportunity does not mean identical opportunity. Children and young people vary in their ability to take advantage of opportunity. Consequently, we must have different kinds of education for different kinds of people.

For younger boys and girls, the common program of elementary education is capable of sufficient differentiation to serve pupils of various abilities. For boys and girls of high-school age, however, a variety of courses is desirable. Equality of educational opportunity means differentiation of educational opportunity. There should be a number of different courses or curricula in secondary schools and colleges designed for people with different abilities and different vocational goals. The high school should offer commercial, homemaking, mechanical arts, agriculture, and college-preparatory courses.

All these differentiated courses should have a substantial common core of "education for the common life." A third to a half of the school day should be spent in this part of the program, with all kinds of students thrown together. In this common core there should be no sectioning of students by vocational aim or social position. But students should be segregated by ability and by vocational aim in the differentiated part of the educational program.

The chief problem which arises in this kind of program is that of placing students in the courses to which they are best adapted. Inevitably, some courses or curricula will have more social prestige than others, and boys and girls, egged on by their parents and by teachers also, will seek admission to the preferred curricula. Nearly all students who desire social recognition now go into a college-preparatory course in high school. In a university the distinctions are not so great among curricula, but still the curricula in agriculture and home economics are often thought of as below the social level of other courses of study.

The kind of change in values which we foresee in American life, away from material success and toward more humane and spiritual values, will make this problem easier of solution. The boy who takes auto mechanics because he likes tools and machines and who promises to become a good husband, father, citizen, and worker in his chosen station in life will not be made to feel guilty because he has not aimed for something "higher." The girl who takes high-school home economics and marries this boy will not be made to feel sorry for herself because she did not become a teacher and marry a lawyer. But this change in social values will come slowly, and the problem of guiding boys and girls into the courses to which they are best suited will continue for a long time to be most difficult.

The best solution of this problem seems to lie in establishing a scientific and honest guidance program. The student's aptitudes, abilities, and expectations in life should be assessed and considered by wise and well-trained counselors who should then give the student and his parents their honest and frank advice. If they should advise a boy to take a commercial course, but in spite of this advice he and his parents should insist on his taking a college-preparatory course, the decision of the boy and his parents should be respected. But standards in the college-preparatory course should be rigorously high, and the boy should be required to meet these standards.

If the boy should succeed in this course, the counselors should give their approval and encouragement. If he should fail, they should advise him once more to follow the course they first suggested. Thus there could be no basis for complaint by the boy or his parents that he was not given equal educational opportunity with others.

In a differentiated educational program of this sort, Tom Brown would probably take a college-preparatory course and go on to college where he would take a course in engineering, or business administration, or law. A friend of Tom's who is also of a middle-class family but has not the proper abilities for a college course would be advised to take a commercial or mechanical course in high school. If he accepted this advice, he would probably graduate from high school in Hometown and go into his father's business, or go to work in a garage or factory, and become a well-adjusted and well-liked citizen. If he and his parents resisted the counselor's advice and insisted on the college-preparatory course, he might fail in this course and then pursue the plan originally advised; or he might barely pass the course, barely get into college, and fail in college after a few months. In this case he would knock about from one job to another until he settled down more or less happily into the kind of job he would have scoffed at a few years earlier. Rarely, this kind of boy would surprise the counselor with some hidden ability and ambition. He would succeed in college and in a vocation requiring abilities that the counselor thought he did not possess.

Tom and his middle-class acquaintances can afford to go to college if they want to. But what about Joe Sienkowitz and a number of other able, ambitious, and talented boys and girls whose parents can barely afford to keep them in high school and cannot hope to send them to college? What does the phrase "equality of educational opportunity" imply in such cases?

Thomas Jefferson faced this same problem in considering an educational program for the state of Virginia a hundred and fifty years ago. Our proposals are essentially the same as Jefferson's when applied to modern conditions. He wrote concerning a proposed law:

This bill proposes to lay off every county into small districts of five or six miles square, called hundreds, and in each of them to establish a school for teaching reading, writing, and arithmetic. The tutor to be supported by the hundred, and every person in it entitled to send their children three years gratis, and as much longer as they please, paying for it. These schools to be under a visitor who is annually to choose the boy of best genius in the school, of those whose parents are too poor to give further education, and to send him forward to one of the grammar schools, of which twenty are proposed to be erected in different parts of the country, for teaching Greek, Latin, geography and the higher branches of numerical arithmetic.

Of the boys thus sent in one year, trial is to be made at the grammar schools one or two years, and the best genius of the whole selected and continued for six years, and the residue dismissed. By this means twenty of the best geniuses will be raked from the rubbish annually, and be instructed at the public expense so far as the grammar schools go. At the end of the six years' instruction, one half are to be discontinued (from among whom the grammar schools will probably be supplied with future masters); and the other half, who are to be chosen for the superiority of their parts and disposition, are to be sent and continued three years in the study of such sciences as they shall choose at William and Mary College. . . .

The general objects of this law are to provide an education adapted to the years, to the capacity, and to the condition of every one, and directed to their freedom and happiness. . . . By that part of our plan which prescribes the selection of youths of genius from among the classes of the poor, we hope to avail the state of these talents, which nature has sown as liberally among the poor as among the rich, but which perish without use if not sought for and cultivated. But of the views of this law none is more important, none more legitimate, than that for rendering the people the safe, as they are the ultimate, guardians of their own liberty. . . .

In every government on earth is some trace of human weakness, some germ of corruption and degeneracy, which cunning will discover and wickedness insensibly open, cultivate, and improve. Every government degenerates when trusted to the rulers of the people alone. The people themselves therefore are its only safe depositories. And to render even them safe, their minds must be improved to a certain degree.[7]

To make educational opportunity effectively equal there must be a broad scholarship program that reaches down into the high school and extends through college and graduate school. Scholarships must be available at the age of fourteen and fifteen when youth begin to drop out of school for financial reasons. The number of scholarships must be large enough to care for some 5 per cent of the boys and girls of high-school age. Such a program will be costly enough to call for support from the federal government.

While careful study and some experience would be necessary in order to determine the number of scholarships that should be provided, a rough estimate can be easily reached. Scholarships for 5 per cent of the youth of high-school age and 2 or 3 per cent of the youth of college age[8] would go far toward meeting the needs of poor but able students.

The cost of such a scholarship program would be large, but not prohibitive. It would cost approximately as much as was spent by the National Youth Administration about 1938 when its load was greatest.

In order to make a broad scholarship program fair to all, we should have to develop selective methods that are both sound and democratic. With our present ability to diagnose intelligence and other capacities and with the knowledge that our better schools possess of the character and family background of their students, it is possible to do a reasonably good job of selecting boys and girls for scholarship aid at the age of fourteen or fifteen. Of course we could not place major reliance on verbal tests of intelligence, since they favor middle-class children. But there are tests of intelligence and other abilities which do not penalize lower-class youth.

A proposal of this sort is bound to attract the charge that it is undemocratic. Some people resist the thought of selecting a small group to receive special help toward social mobility, no matter how democratic the selective procedure may be. Such people prefer to indulge in the fantasy that the really able and deserving young people can all get an education and get ahead in the world if they will only work hard enough. But the hard fact is that we do not have equal educational opportunity and that many able boys and girls are now denied opportunity through no fault of their own. A scholarship program of the sort that we have described would give Joe Sienkowitz and several other talented and industrious Hometown boys and girls a chance which they otherwise would not get. Such a program would contribute to social solidarity through increasing the amount of social mobility without increasing it too much.

Another major source of educational inequality lies in the disparity of wealth among the several states. Such wealthy states as New York and California can provide much greater educational opportunity than some of the less fortunate states in the South and the Great Plains. We shall not have real equality of educational opportunity among the various parts of the country until federal grants of money are given to aid education in these less favored states.

The Administration of Education at Elementary, Secondary, and College Levels

The educational administrator makes educational policy and selects and supervises the teaching staff. In performing both of these functions he needs to exercise judgment based on a knowledge of the facts of social life. We shall consider the work of four groups of educational administrators from this point of view.

a. *The superintendent of schools.* Primarily, the superintendent of schools must teach his school board and his community a democratic educational philosophy which takes account of the facts of social life. If he finds that large sections of the community think of the school only as an instrument for securing social mobility, he must demonstrate to these people that there are other functions of a school system equally important for them and for their children. He must learn the wants of people of various statuses, and he must interpret to them the wants of other people. He must be equally at home in the Rotary Club and the labor unions, with storekeepers and working mothers.

The superintendent also needs to understand the part that status plays in the lives of the people on his staff. The school staff is a hierarchy, a fact of which most teachers are acutely aware. Furthermore, teachers have their own status in the social system of the community, which is affected by their position in the school hierarchy. For example, a teacher who is "demoted" from high-school to elementary-school teaching may happen to be a married woman who, with her husband, is struggling to rise to a secure middle-class position in the community. The change in her status in the school hierarchy might be such a threat to her social status as to cause her severe anxiety and to interfere with her work as a teacher. Another teacher, who is transferred from a high school to an elementary school in a poor neighborhood, may happen to be a woman of secure upper-class status in the community who actually welcomes a chance to work with younger children of low status because it gives her a chance to be philanthropic. Situations like these the superintendent must understand, or he will fail to get the best service out of his staff.

The hierarchy within a school system often functions so autocratically as to snuff out all the initiative and originality of teachers who are low in the system. More than one superintendent makes speeches about the teaching of democracy in his schools while he heads an autocratic regime which intimidates and strait-jackets the classroom teachers. While a hierarchy is inevitable in a school system, it can be a democratic hierarchy.

b. *The elementary school principal.* The principal should be a wise and tolerant person. He has more to do with lower-class parents than any other administrator in the school system. He should understand lower-class morality and see its good points as well as its bad features. It is his job to show his teachers how to do their very best with Joe Sienkowitz, Bob Jones, Katherine Green, and Martha Totten.

The elementary school principal can help his teachers understand the facts of social class. If the teachers, as is usually the case, exhibit a good deal of unconscious discrimination against lower-class children, the principal should make the teachers realize what they are doing. He has to make the school a place where all kinds of children learn to live and work happily together. At the same time, the principal has to see to it that all children with talent and ability are stimulated and encouraged to mount the educational ladder.

c. *The secondary-school principal.* The guidance problem is the secondary-school principal's chief problem in making the school program fair to all. He must develop a group of teachers with guidance responsibilities who know what they have to do, who can deal honestly yet diplomatically with students and their parents, and who have the best scientific techniques of guidance at their command. It is this group of teachers, led by the principal, who must develop and administer a scholarship program that is the only guarantee of equality of opportunity for many students. Again, this group of teachers and the principal must learn how to deal with parents of various social statuses in order to keep the confidence and co-operation of all.

The secondary-school principal and his staff must work out a school program that provides the common education and common experience which are desirable for all students and yet provides the differentiated education which is also essential. He must take the lead in this matter, showing his teachers that administrative difficulties need not get in the way.

d. *The college administrator.* The college dean or college president needs to understand the part that social status and social mobility play in the lives of his students. He may be dealing with students who come from middle- and upper-class families and are assured of maintaining their status. Or he may be dealing with lower-class students who are working to rise in the social scale. Or he may have both types of student on his campus. Especially in the guidance and advisory program of the college should these matters be considered. No student can be helped by a counselor if he is thought of merely as a combination of abilities. His social past and his social goals must come in for consideration. The college administrator should have a clear picture of where his institution fits into the social system, what social groups it serves, and how it can serve these groups in promoting democracy and social solidarity.

The Selection and Education of Teachers

Teachers should know the facts of social structure in America. They should understand the effects of social status upon their pupils and upon themselves. These facts are truly the "facts of life" as far as social life is concerned, and the teacher who is ignorant of them may unwittingly do much harm as well as miss many opportunities of helping children.

Teachers should be aware of the social functions of education. They should know how the school in which they serve actually works to fit boys and girls into American life. If they combine this knowledge with a democratic theory of education and a firm belief in democratic values, they can be effective agents for the maintenance of American democratic society.

They will have increasingly to make decisions affecting the lives of their pupils—to decide who shall receive scholarship help and be aided to develop certain complex abilities and who shall be aided to accept their present social positions and to develop their abilities in order to get maximum enjoyment out of their present stations in life. They will have to understand human needs and human behavior well enough to plan a school program which gives the greatest opportunity for self-realization within the limits of democratic social life.

From what social classes should our teachers be selected? There is a case for selecting teachers of the same social status as their pupils. A teacher from the Bronx for Bronx children. A middle-class teacher for a metropolitan suburb. An Irish Catholic lower-middle class teacher for Irish Catholic city children. A farmer's daughter for a rural school. To state this thesis is to invite one of the hottest fights that educators are capable of waging. The popular conviction on this point is that the teacher should represent standard American manners and morals and speech habits, which is to say that the teacher should be middle-class with the dominant local pronunciation and religious belief. And it seems immoral to many people to suggest that a Polish-American teacher should teach Polish-American children, or a Spanish-American (Mexican) teacher should teach Spanish-American (Mexican) children. Yet the teacher with a background similar to that of his students has the best chance of understanding them, of knowing what their motivations are, and of dealing with their parents.

On the other hand, there is a strong case for selecting teachers from the upper class. The upper-class woman, more often secure and sure of herself in all social situations, can become an excellent teacher. She can afford to be tolerant of things in children which would worry a middle-class person. As has been pointed out, upper-class people are closer to lower-class than to middle-class people in certain characteristics and may therefore be better able to give the lower-class child the encouragement and understanding which are too often bestowed only on middle-class children.

Middle-class teachers tend to bring to their classrooms a middle-class ideology of individual progress and betterment. Children like Bob Jones, who are not actuated by this ideology, rank low in the teachers' esteem. Many of Bob's teachers are worried about the satisfaction that he seems to feel about his lot. They would feel better if he showed more anxiety to get ahead, like Martha Totten. They feel bad if they fail to arouse in their students the social ambitions of which they consider the students worthy. These middle-class teachers may learn that such activities as play, music, arts and crafts, gardening, and photography can give emotional satisfactions, but they carry a fundamental doubt about the rightness of these activities because they contribute to the satisfaction of the individual in his present social position and remove from him the anxiety that leads to social striving.[9]

These middle-class teachers are usually good teachers, but they will do their work better if they learn to look on the values of their own social class as less than God-given. Teacher-training institutions should put them into situations where they have emotionally satisfying experiences in arts and crafts, drama, music, and the like. At the same time, the prospective teachers should be taught to distinguish the basic democratic values of our society from the host of lesser class-bound values which are not a necessary part of a public educational program.

With so much to be said both for and against a policy of selecting teachers from almost any social class, it seems wise to suggest merely that teachers should be selected from a somewhat wider range in the social scale and not bunched so much at the middle. But always it should be remembered that social class is only one of several significant factors in a teacher's personality. We have described three middle-class teachers. Virginia Crane, Helen Bond, and Flora Belle Bennett have three different personalities. Social status should not be the determining factor in selecting teachers; but it certainly is one of the important factors in a teacher's qualifications for the job.

Teachers should participate more in the life of the community in which they teach. This statement does not mean merely that teachers should teach a Sunday-school class and sing in the church choir. It means that teachers should *live* the life of their community. They should take their pleasure in the community as well as give their services. Teachers should not be isolated. We cannot afford to have teachers who are barred from living like other people. It is not good for children to be taught by such people. Why should teachers have to be more "proper" than parents? Parents are not models of morality at all times. Even middle-class parents do many things which are bad examples for their children —things of which they would disapprove in a teacher. In some societies, such as that of early China, a teacher taught a boy to become a man of the world. The teacher had more freedom and was supposed to be more sophisticated than the parents of the community.

In return for freedom to live their own lives, teachers must take more responsibility for social participation. If they are socially in the community, they will tend to be physically in it. They will spend more weekends and more vacations in the community.

When all is said and done, the teacher will inevitably be an exemplar for the class with the most social energy. At the present time in America, that is the middle class. An upper-class teacher will have to stand for middle-class values most of the time, even if she does not believe in them very strongly. A lower-middle class teacher from an immigrant family will strive for upward mobility and therefore will set high value on middle-class behavior wherever he goes.

Unless the middle-class values change in America, we must expect the influence of the schools to favor the values of material success, individual striving, thrift, and social mobility. But there is reason to hope that middle-class values may become more humane and spiritual. Friendliness, co-operativeness, tolerance, love of beauty may be more highly valued. The teacher will then be selected and educated to exemplify these values.

Acknowledgements

The authors wish to acknowledge the valuable assistance of colleagues and friends who aided us in writing this book. Lieutenant Buford Junker, now of the Office of Strategic Services, was most helpful in gathering some of the material. We are particularly grateful to him, John Flint, Arthur S. Hill of the Des Moines Public Schools, and Bernice Neugarten of the University of Chicago for the original data on the schools of Hometown. Celia McCall of Alabama State College for Women, at Montevallo, and the authors of *Deep South*, Mr. and Mrs. Burleigh Gardner and Allison Davis, supplied us with fresh material on the schools of the South. Our colleague and friend, Allison Davis, also greatly aided us with the preparation of part of the chapter on Negro schools. Caroline Tryon and Flora Rhind read the manuscript and offered many useful criticisms. We wish to thank Mildred Hall Warner who helped us edit the book.

To all of these we express our deep appreciation and warm gratitude.

W. Lloyd Warner
Robert J. Havighurst
Martin Loeb

Footnotes

CHAPTER I

Learning for Living

1. This simple view of learning does not account for a small but important set of cases in which children behave as though they wanted to be punished and therefore insist on learning certain things for which they will be punished and refuse to learn other things for which they will be rewarded. This kind of contrary behavior may result from a conflict among the impulses of the child, or it may occur in a child who has a guilty conscience which forces him to seek punishment for relief. To account for learning behavior of this kind we need a complete and refined theory of personality structure and development. For the purposes of this book, however, we shall not need such a theory because we shall not be especially concerned with such exceptional learning behavior.

2. Katherine's experience is typical of the experience of Negro children in small cities of the North. But in the large northern cities, a Negro child would grow up more within groups of Negro children. There would be less competition with white children and less experience of being left out of things. On the other hand, there would be more experience of group solidarity among Negro children and much less equality of economic opportunity. In the South a Negro child would grow up almost entirely within a Negro group, and his only contact with white children would be through conflicts with them. Economic opportunity would be highly restricted. Further discussion of Negro education can be found in Chapter X.

CHAPTER IV

The School in the Status System

1. These figures are based on enrollment figures for school and college appearing in the Biennial Surveys of the United States Office of Education.

2. Harlan Updegraff, *Inventory of Youth in Pennsylvania*. (Washington: American Youth Commission, American Council on Education, 1936. Mimeographed) Data used here are taken from Tables 3, 4, 5, 6, and 14 of the Appendix. Names of pupils were obtained from the sixth-grade rolls of 1926 in school districts distributed so as to be proportional to the number of public-school pupils enrolled in each of the various types of districts and communities in the state. Data concerning 3,022 of these pupils were available in 1934-35, giving their intelligence quotients, scores on the Chapman-Sims

socio-economic scale, and educational history. There were 910 of these pupils with intelligence quotients of 110 or more. The mean score on the Chapman-Sims scale was 5.0 for the group of 3,022 pupils. Accordingly we shall divide the group of superior intelligence into a subgroup with above-average socio-economic status, as indicated by a Chapman-Sims score of 5 or higher, and a subgroup of below average socio-economic status, as indicated by a Chapman-Sims score of less than 5. The data are presented in Table II. From this table the disadvantage of the group with below-average socio-economic status is at once evident.

3. Socio-economic status is not the same as social class, although in many ways they are the same. Those who study the first emphasize economic criteria such as occupation and income; those who study social class emphasize participation in such social institutions as the family, cliques, associations, and churches within a community and the evaluation and ranking of this behavior by members of the same community. The Chapman-Sims scale takes into account the size of one's library, possession of piano, and other marks of culture, as well as size of house, possession of automobile, telephone, etc. If people were ranked on the basis of socio-economic status, the great majority of them, probably more than four-fifths, would have the same position relative to others that their social class position gives them. Since there have been no studies of education in relation to social class position aside from the few that are reported in this book, we must rely upon the studies of education in relation to socio-economic status for information that certainly is relevant to our interests in this book.

4. Helen B. Goetsch, *Parental Income and College Opportunities*. (Teachers College Contributions to Education, No. 795. New York: Teachers College, Columbia University, 1940.) This group fell within percentiles 86-100 on a state-wide scholastic aptitude test given to high-school seniors. Their I.Q.'s ranged from 117 to 146. In April, 1938, 34.5 per cent were in college full-time. The distribution of parental income for this group was not much different from the income distribution for a cross section of Milwaukee families. The relation of full-time college attendance (as of April, 1938) and parental income is shown in Table III. The median parental income for those who were in college full- or part-time was $1,721, while the median parental income for those not in college was $1,285.

5. Bernard D. Karpinos, "School Attendance as Affected by Prevailing Socio-Economic Factors," *School Review*, 51: 39-49 (January, 1943).

6. Howard M. Bell, *Youth Tell Their Story*, pp. 64 ff. American Council on Education, Washington, D.C., 1938.

7. Harold C. Hand, in *General Education in the American High School* (pp. 17-20), by a Committee of the North Central Association of Colleges and Secondary Schools (Chicago: Scott, Foresman and Company, 1942). This money goes for class dues, club dues, fees for laboratory science, mechanical drawing, woodworking, etc., courses; charges for towels, lockers, and gym clothing; band and orchestra instruments and uniforms; textbooks, workbooks, pencils, ink, paper, etc.; athletic equipment, class dresses, class sweaters, rings, pins, keys, etc.; subscriptions to school yearbooks, newspapers, magazines, etc.; photos for school yearbooks, excursion costs; graduation announcements, photographs, diploma fees, cap and gown rental; and so on.

CHAPTER V

Curricula—Selective Pathways to Success

1. D. Chamberlin, Enid S. Chamberlin, N. E. Drought, and W. E. Scott, *Did They Succeed in College*, A Publication of the Eight-Year Study of the Progressive Education Association. (New York: Harper 1942).

2. The studies reported in Chapter VIII, "Teachers in the Status System," bear out this statement.

3. Robert C. Tryon, "Social-Economic Status as a Determinant of Student Participation in a State University," *Psychological Bulletin*, 38: 563, 1941 (Abstract).

4. Goetsch, *op. cit.*, p. 23. The author also found that the median parental income of youth who pursued a higher education in Milwaukee was $1,604; of youth who went outside of Milwaukee but stayed in Wisconsin, $2,571; and of youth who went outside of Wisconsin, $3,125. In Milwaukee there is Marquette University, the Milwaukee State Teachers College, Milwaukee-Downer College, and a lower division (first two years) of the University of Wisconsin, as well as institutions for training in business, nursing, and industrial trades. Youth who go outside of Milwaukee go to the State University or to one of the church-related liberal arts colleges. Youth who leave the state mainly go to independent colleges and universities, largely in the East.

CHAPTER VI

Status in the Classroom

1. Bernice L. Neugarten, "The Relation Between Family Social Position and the Social Development of the Child," Doctoral Dissertation, University of Chicago Library, 1943.

CHAPTER VIII

Teachers in the Status System

1. There is not much scientific basis for locating farmers in the social class structure, but the ordinary small farmer in the Middle West would participate with upper-lower or lower-middle class people in the neighboring small cities.

2. M'Ledge Moffett, *The Social Background and Activities of Teachers' College Students*, p. 26. Teachers College Contributions to Education, No. 375. (New York: Teachers College, Columbia University, 1929.) It will be noted that the percentages do not total 100 in either table. No explanation is given in the text.

3. *Ibid.*, p. 33.

4. Willard S. Elsbree, *The American Teacher*, p. 555. New York: American Book Company, 1939.

CHAPTER IX

The Administrative Hierarchy

1. Harold C. Hand, "Who Runs our School Boards?" *The American Teacher,* Vol. 23, April, 1939.

George S. Counts, *The Social Composition of Boards of Education,* Table XXIII, p. 52. Chicago: University of Chicago, Supplementary Educational Monographs, No. 33, 1927.

CHAPTER X

The Negro in the American Caste System

1. *Deep South,* pp. 16-17.

2. *Ibid.,* p. 18.

3. Edwin R. Embree, *The American Negro, A Handbook* (New York: John Day, 1942). A recent United States Supreme Court decision requires the states to provide equal pay for Negro and white teachers of equal preparation. This will probably raise the proportion of the educational dollar which the southern states spend on Negro education.

4. The recent Supreme Court decision requires states to provide professional education for Negroes. This is done normally by paying tuition fees for Negro citizens to attend universities which will admit Negroes, often in the North.

5. As has been stated earlier, much less money is spent on the education of a Negro child than is spent on the education of a white child.

6. As the fieldworkers observed the efficiency of many of these more literate tenants, on the one hand, and the confusion of the great mass of illiterate tenants, on the other hand, it seemed clear that a thorough elementary education for colored rural children would increase the chances of their modifying the caste and economic systems. As long as most tenants were illiterate, they could effect no important changes within these systems, nor could they benefit by the efforts of the federal government to modify the economic system.

7. The operation of caste controls upon Negro education is indicated throughout this history of money-raising to buy essential equipment. Adequate equipment of the same type was supplied to the white schools by the school board. The upper-class men in this branch of the Negro P.T.A. commented repeatedly upon this discrimination against their children. Several of them paid more money in taxes annually to the city and county than was required to equip the science laboratory. It was never equipped.

CHAPTER XI

Who Shall Be Educated?

1. F. W. Taussig and C. S. Joslyn, *American Business Leaders*, p. 234. New York: Macmillan Co., 1932.

2. F. W. Taussig and C. S. Joslyn, *American Business Leaders*, p. 103. New York: Macmillan and Co., 1932. It should be remembered in interpreting this table that the proportion of farmers in the population has been decreasing, but even when allowance is made for this decrease, the farmers' sons are seen to be rising less frequently to the top business positions, while sons of business leaders assume these positions more frequently.

3. National Resources Committee, *The Problems of a Changing Population*, pp. 139 ff. Washington: Government Printing Office, 1938.

4. J. J. Osborn, "The Vanishing Race of Princetonians," *Princeton Alumni Weekly*, XL:45-48 (1939).

5. The problem of religious teaching in the public schools is a difficult one. Where a society has a common religion, this religion is taught in the schools and religious instruction is definitely an instrument for producing social solidarity. But Americans are not united by common religious beliefs except in the broad sense that democratic ideals coincide in a general way with some of our religious ideals. In America, it is the privilege and duty of the family to care for the religious education of children. Families band together in churches and thus achieve a limited amount of social solidarity. But we must rely on other things than religion for solidarity on a national scale.

6. Educational Policies Commission, *Learning the Ways of Democracy*, Washington, D. C., National Education Association, 1940.

7. Thomas Jefferson, *Notes on Virginia*, pp. 147-151. Baltimore: W. Pechin, 1800.

8. It is well-known that many colleges have scholarship funds and that a few colleges have really large funds. At Harvard College, perhaps one boy in five receives scholarship aid. But few colleges approach this mark. On the other hand, about half the university students in Great Britain receive scholarship help.

9. Roger G. Barker, "Difficulties of Communication Between Educators and Psychologists: Some Speculations," *Journal of Educational Psychology*, 34: 416-426 (September, 1942). The author has developed these ideas in a highly suggestive way in this paper.

Working Bibliography

The purposes of this bibliography are (1) to give the reader the principal sources of our evidence and (2) to provide instructors and others with the necessary material to obtain a fuller understanding of this book's central problems. It is not designed as an exhaustive coverage of all that has been written on the subject. We believe each book or article listed is of basic importance as evidence and for background.

The publications are classified by chapters. When necessary, selections are indicated by page references. One book may be cited several times because of its significance for several chapters.

CHAPTER I. LEARNING FOR LIVING

Background reading for this chapter consists mainly of studies of the social orientation of children and studies of the learning process. Studies of the social status system of American communities should also be read in this connection. These studies are listed in the notes on Chapters II and X. The following studies of social orientation and social learning are recommended:
Social Learning and Imitation—Neal A. Miller and John Dollard. New Haven: Yale University Press, 1941. This book explains the process of learning by imitation and accounts for much of the informal learning of children as imitation.
"American Status Systems and the Socialization of the Child"—Allison Davis. *American Sociological Review*, 6:345-356 (June, 1941). This study discusses the role of age, sex, and social class position in the socialization of the human organism.
"Child Socialization and the School"—Robert J. Havighurst and Allison Davis. *Review of Educational Research*, 13:29-37 (February, 1943). States a theory of social development and summarizes recent research on this subject.

CHAPTER II. AMERICAN STATUS SYSTEMS

The evidence for this chapter comes from several studies of American communities. The principal ones are:
The Social Life of a Modern Community, Vol. I: The Yankee City Series—W. Lloyd Warner and Paul S. Lunt. New Haven: Yale University Press, 1941.

The Status System of a Modern Community, Vol. II: The Yankee City Series—W. Lloyd Warner and Paul S. Lunt. New Haven: Yale University Press, 1942. These two volumes (four more are to be published) describe the status system of a New England community. Pages 422 to 451 of Vol. I, which summarize the principal features of Yankee City, should be read for this chapter.

Deep South—Allison Davis, Burleigh Gardner, and Mary R. Gardner. Chicago: University of Chicago Press, 1941. Reports on Old City in the Deep South. Pages 59 to 255 provide some of the necessary background to understand the class system of southern whites.

Caste and Class in a Southern Town—John Dollard. New Haven: Yale University Press, 1937. Gives a detailed analysis of life in a small southern town. It also analyzes personality adjustment to the status system.

Life, Liberty and Property—Alfred Winslow Jones, Philadelphia: Lippincott, 1941. Provides a systematic analysis of the class ideology of a small city in the Middle West.

Middletown in Transition—Robert and Helen Lynd. New York: Harcourt, Brace & Company, 1937. Indicates some of the changes that have occurred in the status system in the Middle West in the last ten years.

Hometown—John Flint. (Mimeographed copies are in the library of the Committee on Human Development, University of Chicago.) Studies the status system of a midwestern town and its relation to the school system.

Gold Coast and the Slum—Harvey Warren Zorbaugh. Chicago: University of Chicago Press, 1929. Gives a clear picture of how the status system operates in Chicago.

The Material Culture and Social Institutions of the Simpler Peoples—L. T. Hobhouse, G. C. Wheeler, and M. Ginsberg. London: Chapman and Hall, 1915. A systematic analysis of the relation of social complexity to technological advancement. It provides evidence which indicates how social class and other status systems are closely allied to technological advancement.

CHAPTER III. SOCIAL MOBILITY—GOING UP AND COMING DOWN

Social scientists have done little to study American social mobility. This task has been left largely to the writers. The output of the latter ranges from the naïve acceptance of the conventional ideology of the success story found in our popular magazines to serious analyses of life careers expressive of upward and downward mobility. We will cite but a few of the latter variety.

The works of John P. Marquand, particularly *Wickford Point, The Late George Apley*, and *So Little Time*, describe the behavior of the top layers of New England society. Some of the material he uses sounds strangely as if it might have come from the community described in the Yankee City Series. He is particularly apt in drawing realistic accounts of upper-upper people in relation to mobile individuals from the lower-upper class.

Christopher La Farge's *The Wilsons*, some of which appeared in the *New Yorker*, is an analysis of the efforts of a lower-upper woman to get into top society in a New England city. The effect on her children is well-drawn.

Christopher Morley's *Kitty Foyle* describes the relationships of the Philadelphia Main Liners to those beneath them.

Sinclair Lewis' *Babbitt* gives a good account of the social classes in a small midwestern city.

Booth Tarkington's *Alice Adams* should be read. It tells of the efforts of a middle-class girl and her family to gain acceptance by those above them.

From *Yankee City* the profiles of the Starr family (pages 141 to 152), Delgracia (pages 161 to 168), the Stanleys (pages 188 to 193), and the Dixons (pages 193 to 196) should be read. They illustrate several kinds of social mobility for several social levels.

Margaret Mead's *And Keep Your Powder Dry* (New York: Morrow, 1942) analyzes the American people's belief in success.

Pitirim Sorokin's *Social Mobility* (New York: Harper, 1927) gives some of the ideas held by social scientists on social hierarchies.

CHAPTER IV. THE SCHOOL IN THE STATUS SYSTEM

In recent years there has been a good deal of study of the school as a social institution and its changing functions in relation to the home, industry, agriculture, and other social institutions. As general reading in this area, the following books are suggested:

Community Backgrounds of Education—Lloyd A. Cook. New York: McGraw-Hill Book Company, 1938. This book gives a good general overview of various types of communities and of the social forces shaping the child. It is recommended as background reading in educational sociology.

General Education in the American High School.—A committee of the North Central Association of Colleges and Secondary Schools. Chicago: Scott, Foresman and Company, 1942. This book summarizes the development of the American high school and shows how it functions in present-day society. In connection with this chapter, chapters 1, 2, 3, 4, and 6 should be read.

The National Survey of Secondary Education. The Secondary School Population—Grayson N. Kefauver, Victor H. Noll, and C. Ellwood Drake. Washington, D.C. Bulletin of the U.S. Office of Education, 1932, No. 17. Gives data on the selectivity of the American high school in 1930.

The Selective Character of American Education—George S. Counts. Chicago: Department of Education, University of Chicago, 1922. Supplementary Educational Monographs, No. 19. Shows how parental occupation was related to high-school attendance and to choice of course of study about 1920.

CHAPTER V. CURRICULA—SELECTIVE PATHWAYS TO SUCCESS

CHAPTER VI. STATUS IN THE CLASSROOM

These chapters are based largely upon the researches in Yankee City, Old City, and Hometown. The reader should see the chapters on "Social Mobility" and "The Class Systems of Negroes and Whites" in *Deep South*; and pages 188 to 196 of Vol. I of the Yankee City Series should be read. For more detailed information see:

"Social Status and Education in a Southern Community"—Burleigh B. Gardner, Mary R. Gardner, and Martin B. Loeb.—*School Review*, 50:179-191 (March, 1942).

"The School and Social Structure in a Midwestern Community"—Buford H. Junker, and Martin B. Loeb.—*School Review*, 50: 686-695 (December, 1942).

CHAPTER VII. SOCIAL MOBILITY THROUGH EDUCATION

The typical American success stories in our popular magazines and novels should be read and compared with Martha's life career and those described in Chapter II.

CHAPTER VIII. TEACHERS IN THE STATUS SYSTEM

The material for this chapter is drawn mainly from the files of the Yankee City, Old City, and Hometown researches. There are a number of published biographies of schoolteachers, some of them fictionalized, in which the reader will find life stories similar to those of the two teachers described in this chapter. Material on the community participation of teachers is summarized in:
Community Contacts and Participation of Teachers—Florence Greenhoe. Washington, D.C. American Council on Public Affairs, 1941.

CHAPTER IX. THE ADMINISTRATIVE HIERARCHY

Most of the material in this chapter comes from the research in Yankee City. This material has not previously been published. In addition to the case studies from Yankee City, we have drawn on published studies of the social composition of school boards.

CHAPTER X. THE NEGRO IN THE AMERICAN CASTE SYSTEM

There is an extensive bibliography on the social place of the Negro in America, particularly in the South. The works of Franklin Frazier, Charles S. Johnson, Robert Park, Guy Johnson, Horace Mann Bond, and Howard W. Odum, among others, should be consulted. The publications listed here are of special significance to the thesis of this chapter.
Children of Bondage—Allison Davis and John Dollard, 1940.
Growing Up in the Black Belt—Charles S. Johnson, 1940.
Negro Youth at the Crossways—Franklin Frazier, 1940.
Color and Human Nature—W. Lloyd Warner, Buford Junker, and Walter Adams, 1941.
Color, Class, and Personality—Robert L. Sutherland, 1942.
All the above books, published by the American Council on Education, Washington, D.C., deal with the problem of how Negro children grow up in our American status system. The books of Davis and Dollard and Johnson are about the South, Frazier writes about the border states, and Warner, Junker, and Adams about Chicago. Sutherland's book generalizes on the findings of the others.
American Negroes—a handbook by Edwin M. Embree (New York: John Day, 1942), gives in readable form most of the significant statistics on how discrimination works to the disadvantage of the Negro.

Brown Americans—Edwin Embree (New York: Viking Press, 1943), provides excellent background on Negro life.
Deep South—Allison Davis, Burleigh Gardner, and Mary R. Gardner. Chicago: University of Chicago Press, 1941. Pages 3 to 59 describe the system of color castes in the South.

CHAPTER XI. WHO SHALL BE EDUCATED

Many books and articles have been written on the relation of education to democracy, and we can single out only a few that deal especially with the subjects of social mobility and social solidarity in relation to education and to the welfare of our democratic society. We shall also cite several studies of the problems of young people as a group in our society.
Youth and the Future—The American Youth Commission. Washington, D.C.: The American Council on Education, 1942. This is the final report of the American Youth Commission. It summarizes the place of youth during the 1930's and proposes a program for meeting the problems of youth.
Equal Educational Opportunity for Youth—Newton Edwards. Washington, D.C.: The American Council on Education, 1939. Here the author brings together the facts about inequality of educational support and educational facilities among the various states.
Barriers to Youth Employment—Paul T. David. Washington, D.C.: The American Council on Education, 1942. This is a clear analysis of the economic life of young people in America, and shows the nature of the barriers which stand in the way of economic achievement by young people.
Youth Tell Their Story—Howard M. Bell. Washington, D.C.: The American Council on Education, 1938. A summary of the problems and the sentiments of a cross section of American youth in the 1930's.
New Adventures in Democracy—Ordway Tead. New York: McGraw-Hill Book Company, 1939. This book deals with the general problem of making education, public service, and industry truly democratic. Of special interest are chapters 6 and 7, dealing with the problem of vocational orientation and opportunity; chapter 9, treating problems of securing well-trained people for public service; and chapter 16, the problem of leadership in a democracy.
"Education for a Classless Society"—James B. Conant: Atlantic Monthly, 165: 593-602 (May, 1940). The President of Harvard University argues for social mobility through education.
And Keep Your Powder Dry—Margaret Mead. New York: Morrow, 1942. Miss Mead's analysis of American character in relation to social mobility has important implications for education.
Education for Social Cohesion in a Democracy—Robert J. Havighurst, pp. 18-41 in *Education in a Democracy*, edited by Newton Edwards. Chicago: University of Chicago Press, 1941. Analyzes the problem of education in relation to social solidarity, and proposes an educational program.
The New Vision—L. Maholy-Nagy. New York: W. W. Norton & Co., 1938. The former member of the Bauhaus in Germany and present director of the New School of Design in Chicago discusses new goals and ways of learning in the arts and their importance to society.
Unemployment in the Learned Professions—Walter M. Kotschnigg. London: Oxford University Press, 1937. Describes the overcrowding of the pro-

fessions in Europe after the First World War when universities expanded and took many more students than could find positions in that society. "The Economic Stratification of Youth and Its Social Consequences"—A. C. Rosander. *Journal of Educational Psychology*, 32: 592-604 (April, 1939). Reports on studies of the relation of parental occupation to school attendance and choice of occupation by sons and daughters.

The Dynamics of Population—Frank Lorimer and Frederick Osborn. New York: Macmillan, 1934. See especially chapter IV for data on the differential fertility of various classes of the population.

"The Teacher as a Transmitter of Culture"—Mark A. May. *Educational Administration and Supervision*, 26: 161-175 (March, 1940). Argues that the teacher should be a good specimen of his culture and particularly of the subculture in which he expects to teach.

Index

American Federation of Teachers, 109

Birth rates, 153-155
Board of Education, 65, 115. *See also* School Board

Caste, 18, 19
American caste system, 120-123
role of the school in, 137, 138
See also Negro
Character, 143
Class, social, 18-32, 123-124, 144
in American communities, 20
and children's reputations, 85-87
definition of, 19
Negro class order, 123-124
and parental training, 87
regional differences, 29, 31
and the school, 83, 107
See also Status systems; Upper class; Middle class; Lower class
Class attitudes, 5, 9-10, 26
child-child, 5-6, 82, 85-86
Class discriminations, 76
by children, 82, 83, 85-86
by teachers, 81, 95, 168
College, and the status system, 71-72
college-preparatory courses, 64, 68, 161
functions of, 55, 56, 161
growth in enrollment, 48
as a selective agency, 51, 151
and social mobility, 48
social status of college students, 52-53, 59, 66
who attends, 52-53, 59, 66, 131
Curricula, 58-72, 142, 163
college curriculum and parental income, 72
in Old City high school, 58
proposals for, 158-162
and social status, 61-62
"undifferentiated," 69-70

Curricula—*Continued*
in Yankee City high school, 60, 78-79

Deep South
caste system of, 120-123
class system of, 27-28
See also Old City
Democracy, 16, 55, 68, 69, 70, 158
education for democracy, 141-144, 148, 158, 159, 160
in education for Negroes, 138-140

Economic status, and educational opportunity, 50-53
of Negroes, 135-136
of Negro teachers, 134
and social status, 124, 144, 176
Economic mobility, 152-153
Economic improvement and moral improvement, 155
Education, and class position, 67
for democracy, 141-144, 148
equality of opportunity for, 51-54, 162, 164-165
of Negroes (*see* Negro education)
proposed educational program, 158-172
for social change, 143
and social mobility, 47-49, 56-57, 61, 88-97
and the status system, 56
See also School
Educational policy, and administration, 167-169
content of the educational program, 158-162; *See also* Curriculum
organization of the educational program, 162-167
scholarships, 165-166, 168
selection and education of teachers, 169-172
See also Education